Easy Bulletin Boards

Number 2

by

MELVYN K. BOWERS

D1367528

The Scarecrow Press, Inc.
Metuchen, N.J.   1974

Library of Congress Cataloging in Publication Data

Bowers, Melvyn K
  Easy bulletin boards, number 2.

  1. Bulletin boards. I. Title.
LB1045.B666   371.33'56   73-21798
ISBN 0-8108-0695-9

To everyone who helped--

My young friends and Library Aides
Sally, who typed and found errors
Lynn, who kept my work area clean
My wife, who protected me from interruptions
Keith, who did some of my work for me
And to Charlie, who did nothing but bark.

PREFACE

During the past few years, informative bulletin boards and "teaching" boards with clear, meaningful lettering and attractive illustrations have become a "must" throughout the school system.

Much of the professional literature today offers designs for this purpose, and there are a number of publications dealing with this subject. While most of these offer excellent ideas, many are too time consuming to construct, or use materials that are not usually at hand.

In this, his most recent publication, Mr. Bowers has shown a range of interesting and original bulletin boards. Though designed primarily for the library, most of them could be adapted to many classroom uses as well. Of greatest value to the busy teacher or librarian is the fact that all the designs can be quickly and easily completed, and require materials that are easily obtained. Elaborate, expensive, time-consuming bulletin boards are no longer necessary when ideas that are simple and easily understood are so readily at hand, in a book such as this one.

Grace E. Bonebright
Principal
East Lake School

TABLE OF CONTENTS

Part I: The Basics

Part II: Design Ideas

Part I

BASICS

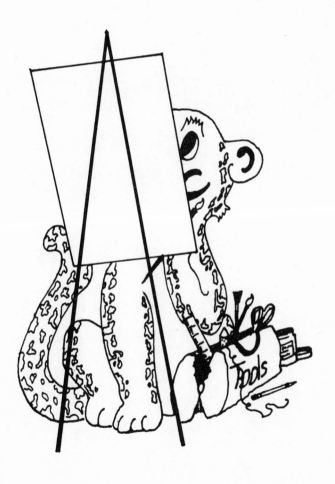

Chapter 1

THE LIBRARIAN'S TOOL KIT

On a bottom shelf in an out-of-the-way corner of the book storage room is an old and faded canvas overnight bag. It has a few holes in it, and the zipper hasn't worked for years, but the ancient bag is invaluable when a display is to be constructed for it contains the tools that will probably be needed.

There is a small pair of tin snips, ten-inch shears, a pair of six-inch pointed scissors and an X-acto knife with two or three extra blades. These tools serve the required cutting and trimming needs except for what is done on the paper cutter.

A bottle of white glue, scotch tape, masking tape, double-faced tape, a small block of photographer's wax, Stik-Taks, a small stapler, a tub of common pins, and a few pins with colored heads satisfy most of the joining and mounting needs.

Layouts are done with a small carpenter's tape, a dime store triangle and a twelve-inch ruler. A three-foot length of string serves both as a compass and as a level line for laying out horizontal lines. Another length of string has a fishing weight fastened to one end. This serves as a plumb to guide vertical lines. There is also a yard stick, but that is too big to fit into the bag.

A box of assorted crayons, an assortment of colored felt-tip pens with various sizes of tips, two or three water-color brushes, a bottle of black ink, and three pigment mixing tins serve most of the coloring requirements.

A pair of needlenose pliers, a pair of side cutters and a small tack hammer complete the collection.

Since the tools were all acquired at the dime store

or at some sale, the kit represents an investment of under
five dollars.   The mention of the old overnight bag was intended to point out that more elaborate storage kits are unnecessary.

These tools are always kept together in the bag.
Borrowing is discouraged for there is always the possibility
of their not being returned to their proper place, and time
is lost searching for them or acquiring replacements.

Near the bag of tools stands a fair-sized cardboard
carton.   At any moment this box will contain such things as
construction paper, colored wrapping papers, a wallpaper
sample book, scraps of yardage, netting, colored yarn, tissue paper, paper plates and other "goodies" that are picked
up from time to time and are usable in making letters and
objects for a display.   It is a constant chore to keep the box
full of a wide assortment of materials for teachers and
children are always browsing for a bit or piece of something
needed in their work.

On a shelf, stored in plastic bags to keep them clean,
are a few models children have given to the library and are
used from time to time in displays and occasionally borrowed by a teacher for class use.   There are also a few
sprigs of plastic greenery and some plastic flowers and
leaves in fall colors.   Letters and flat objects that are
stored for future use are kept in manila envelopes.   Saving
these kinds of things may save some time in constructing
a display, but they do need occasional weeding.

An old filing cabinet rescued from the dump is also
in the storage room.   This is used to file dust jackets to
be used in display work and for classroom circulation.   The
dust jackets are first trimmed of any unnecessary paper.
The notes concerning the author, illustrator, or a story sum-
mary are trimmed, mounted on tagboard and filed with the
dust jacket.

Filing is done by subject headings, keeping the number of headings to a minimum.   The contents of the collection will vary from time to time as new materials are
added and the old are weeded out.

The above-mentioned tools and materials do not in-
clude all those that may appear in the collection from time
to time, and they are not intended to represent a complete

listing of all the possibilities. They do serve to indicate the variety of materials and the value of having such a collection readily available when it is time to construct a new display for the library.

Chapter 2

MATERIALS

We are surrounded in our every day environment by
a wealth of material suitable for display purposes, the only
limitations being space, time for utilization, and the librarian's imagination and creative instincts.

One high school had a wrecked automobile outside
the auto shop with a display of book jackets and descriptive
materials advertising safety, highway engineering, driving and
related topics. It was very effective.

While most librarians would not care to drag in an
old wrecked auto, the incident helps point out the vast array
of materials that could be used in display work.

Rather than offer a catalog of materials that would
probably prove useless, this chapter includes some special
handling problems, and the use of a few common and adaptable materials that are very often overlooked.

Special Handling Problems

Some materials require special handling in display
work. From time to time it may be desirable to use items
of value, or which may not be replaceable should damage
or loss occur. A doll display may contain an antique, or
one of personal value. Old books, relics from our past
history, some hobby collections and works of art or handi-
crafts are a few examples. These items should be displayed
in locked cabinets or windows where they may be seen but
not handled, and damage or loss is less likely to occur.
When possible, a model of the object or a reprint may be
just as satisfactory as the original, and save worry.

Materials of value offered for display by friends of
the library should only be accepted with the understanding

that the library staff will take all possible precautions to
safeguard the material, but cannot be responsible beyond
reasonable care. The wise librarian will discuss such
loans with his administrator before accepting them, and it
may be well to have such loans covered in the school
policies.

One possible alternative to such loans might be to
construct related displays for the library, and invite the
friend to visit the library and show his material. Such an
afternoon is almost always interesting to the children, cer-
tainly of value, and relieves the library and librarian of the
responsibility for care and maintenance.

It is always possible that children may bring something to the library for display which the parents would
rather be kept at home. If a suspect item should turn up
in the library, it is good procedure to consult with the parents before accepting the materials for display purposes.
A telephone call will usually be sufficient, and is good pub-
lic relations.

Caution where valuable or irreplaceable items are
concerned cannot be over-emphasized. A school library
in California accepted a coin collection which was displayed
in a locked glass case. The collection was stolen, and the
school faced a law suit which, fortunately, was averted by
the recovery of the collection.

It may seem redundant to mention such things as
blasting caps, war souvenirs, model rocket engines and
other potentially dangerous items. However, such items,
loaded and fused, have occasionally appeared in displays.
There are occasions to use such items, but extreme caution
must be exercised in being certain that they are completely
disarmed and absolutely harmless.

Displays utilizing attractors such as gingerbread men,
sugar-cube castles or other objects constructed of candies
or simulated goodies must be harmless to protect a small
patron who might find the temptation to nibble greater than
the will to resist. There may be an occasional youngster
the librarian would like to poison, but it is usually best
to grant this privilege to someone else.

Occasionally incense or artificial scent is sprayed on
a plastic bouquet for effect. This practice is fine for home

use, but not for school because some people find such odors
offensive, and a few are allergic to them.   They really add
little to the atmosphere of the design or the library decor.

        Some items, because of their bulk or other physical
characteristics cannot be suspended or mounted by pins or
more common hanging methods.   Sometimes temporary shelving may provide the answer.   These shelves may be built
from boxes or other methods used such as are discussed
later in this chapter.   A more satisfactory method of pro-
viding for temporary shelving when needed is to mount wall
brackets on either side of the space.   When shelving is required, the hangers and shelves are installed in a matter
of moments.   When not needed, they are easily removed
and stored.   The brackets, which remain permanently installed on the wall, are not noticeable and do not detract
from the space in any way.   Brackets, hangers and pre-
finished shelving in a wide variety of sizes may be purchased from lumber yards, hardware stores, furniture
stores and many of the so called "cut-rates."   Experience
has shown that such installations cost under ten dollars,
and it takes only a few minutes for a janitor or someone
from the wood shop to install the brackets alongside the
space.

        Another possible solution, when the library arrange-
ment is such as to make it possible, is to move a table
under the space and arrange the display so the objects may
rest on the table.   It is often difficult to maintain a unity
in such a display, and, unless handling the objects is of no
concern, it is difficult to maintain a hands-off environment.
It is also sometimes difficult to prevent miscellaneous items
being layed on the table and creating an undesirable clutter.

Coat Hangers and Paper Cones

        While the purpose of this book is more to present
ideas than to be just another "how-to-do-it" volume on bulletin boards, there are two common materials that are not
often used which because of their simplicity and versatility
are deserving of some consideration here.

        Wire coat hangers can be used in their existing shape
for a number of purposes, or easily cut with the side cutters and bent into a wide variety of useful shapes.   They
are usable for decorative objects which serve as attractors,

or as furniture to hold a book, magazine, sign, model or bit of realia.

Wire coat hangers used in pairs with a paper plate or construction paper head make excellent representations of people. If more color is desired, the wire coat hangers may be wrapped, or they may be mounted over some colorful surface such as paper or fabric.

When bent into proper shape and necessary details added with some colorful material, a variety of forms take shape.

Wire coat hangers may be bent into functional items of furniture as these few illustrations will demonstrate.

Some more ideas at random:

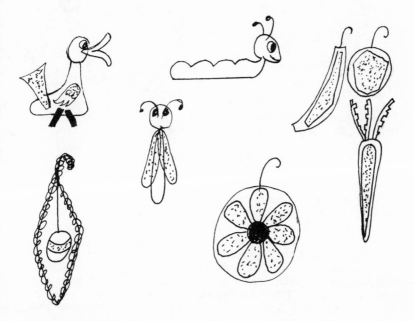

Paper Cones

Paper cones serve many of the same purposes as the coat hangers, are very easy to construct, and have the advantage of built-in color, depending upon the material from which they are constructed.

The basic cone is made simply by rolling up a piece of paper, starting at a corner and rolling diagonally to the opposite corner. The point should be kept quite sharp and

the base allowed to flare out.   The tag end is held in place
by glue, a bit of scotch tape or staple.   The base is then
trimmed both to level it off and to achieve the desired
height.

The simplest form of cone used requires only a basic
cone and a head cut from construction paper, or perhaps
from a book or advertising illustration.   A tail may be
added if desired.   The four illustrations below consisted of
a cone, a paper head cemented to the cone, and in the case
of the cat and turkey, a tail added.

These have an added advantage over the coat hanger in that
they can be made almost any size desired.

More complete figures may be made by adding more
detail.   A hat may be added by simply cutting a circle to
size, cut a small hole in the center and slide it over the
pointed end of the cone.   If the brim doesn't come down far
enough, simply make the center hole a bit larger.   A drop
of glue will help hold it in place.   Arms may be made by
cutting a strip of paper and after lightly curling, cement
it to the back of the figure.

In the illustrations below, the witch has a hat, paper
hair cemented in place before the hat brim was put on, and
a tiny paper cone cemented to her face for a nose.   The little
angel had wings cemented to the back of the cone and a
halo cemented in place.   The crazy bird had a top-knot cut
from scraps of colored paper.   The little girl had a tiny
bunch of miniature flowers cemented to her hat for added
color.   These forms are a bit more time consuming to construct, but they are very attractive, and can be built with
as much detail as patience and time will allow.

These figures are a good project for the children in
the library club who are engaged in bulletin board construction, and might be suggested to teachers searching for an
idea for their art classes.

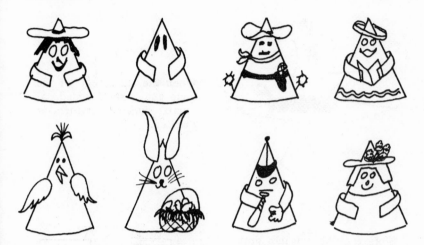

Paper cones are also usable for furniture which can be either mounted in a bulletin board space, or rest on a table or shelf.

These are easily constructed, and very useful.

When part of the cone is cut away it will support a book, magazine or a poster.   It will also hold material open to a given page.

When a shelf is added to the cone it will support a small object and act as a frame to emphasize or attract attention.

When the tip is cut off the cone and a shelf added, a small, durable platform is created.

Slots may be cut into small cones to support a small sign or notice. Posters or book jackets may be mounted to larger cones for support.

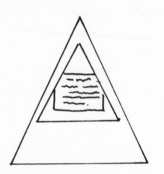

Cutting an opening in a cone and mounting a small notice inside insures the notice being read, for people can not resist taking a peek.

The same idea can be used to create a holiday decoration. The inside of the cone should be painted, or the cone made from two different materials or colors cemented back to back before rolling the cone.

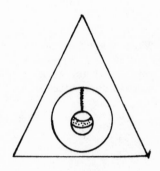

There are many other ideas for using cones and various
paper shapes. Many art books dealing with paper cutting
and paper sculpture will provide a wealth of ideas for the
librarian.

For the reader interested in pursuing the use of materials, the author has found the following list of titles
most helpful.

Pack-O-Fun   Clapper Publishing Co., Inc. 14 Main
           St., Park Ridge, Illinois, 60068.
           This little scrap magazine is published
           monthly except July and August. Sub-
           scription rate at the present is $5.00
           per year. This company also pub-
           lishes some little handbooks on the use
           of specific materials such as their
           Make It with Punched Cards and Fun
           with Macaroni.

Make It with Paper Wood, Louise. David McKay Co.,
           Inc., 750 3rd Ave., New York, 10017.
           List price, $5.95.

Arts and Activities Arts and Activities, 8150 N. Central
           Park Ave., Skokie, Ill., 60076. Pub-
           lished monthly except July and August.
           Subscription rate is $7.00. This
           magazine is probably on your profes-
           sional shelf now, or should be.

Seasonal publications of such magazines as Better
Homes and Gardens, Women's Home Companion, and Mc-
Call's are also useful sources for ideas.

Chapter 3

LETTERING THE BULLETIN BOARD

Some of the suggestions for lettering presented in this chapter may possibly offend the graphic artist or typographer, but precise or artistic lettering is an integral part of his or her profession, rooted in the individual's particular talents and developed during years of training. The librarian may not possess such talent, and his or her training was spent in the acquisition of other skills more closely allied to the varied work of the profession of librarianship.

Since lettering is an integral part of the artist's profession, he uses the necessary time to complete a professional job. The librarian does not have the time to do the same precise drafting or fine art lettering. He must sandwich this work into a day already crowded with the many activities of his profession, some of which may actually be more important to him in reaching his objectives than the particular display he has under construction at the moment.

Yet, the librarian must do a creditable job with his bulletin boards if they are to function as a vital working tool. He can use neither a lack of skill, talent or time as an apology.

The suggestions offered in this chapter are not intended to "teach" the fine art of lettering. The librarian who wishes to develop real skill in this work will find courses offered in the arts or audio-visual departments of a nearby college most helpful. The purpose is to present to those many librarians who have difficulty with lettering a few suggestions that have proven to be adequate for library display purposes, economical in time, and requiring little skill. It is hoped these busy people will find the suggestions helpful.

Criteria

While lettering need not be graphically perfect, it does

require certain qualities to be satisfactory, the principal ones
being listed below with no significance attached as to order
in which they appear.

1.   Lettering must be neat and placed so as to become
     an integral part of the design.
2.   The style of lettering must fit the theme and mood
     of the design.
3.   The caption must be easily read from a reasonable
     distance.
4.   Captions should, at least in the lower elementary
     grades, read from left to right in normal compo-
     sition form.
5.   Style and material should be varied between de-
     signs to prevent monotony.
6.   Lettering should not be used at all when a design
     is able to sell itself, or where the design objec-
     tive is merely to be decorative.

Material

Any material which can be cut, shaped, draped, colored and mounted is suitable for lettering purposes, though
some materials may be easier to work than others. Very
lightweight fabrics, silk and nylon may be difficult to cut and
tend to sag out of shape when mounted unless they are first
cemented to tagboard or heavy paper to act as a stiffening
agent.

Metals, plastics and wood are examples of materials
which are difficult to mount unless they have small holes
drilled through them to receive pins or small nails.   They
can be mounted by pressing thumbtacks along the edges so
the head lays over the material and holds them in place, but
the large heads of the pins may prove unsightly, and the
drilled holes are much more satisfactory.

Lightweight papers such as tissue and cellophane are
easier to cut with an X-acto knife than with shears.   The
material should be laid on a discarded magazine or a few old
newspapers before cutting. Heavy materials, such as carpet-
ing, should be cut with tin snips after the design has been
sketched in reverse on the back side.

Some plastics, metal foil and other material that may
have a highly reflective surface should be used only where
light reflections will create no problems.

Interesting and colorful letters may be made by draping yarn, string, raffia, cord, beads or similar material over pins that have been pressed into the surface so as to outline the desired letters.

Letters may also be painted directly on the background. The medium used must be fairly fast drying, and must not be so thin as to run or drip. Tempera and similar dry pigments should be mixed quite thick to prevent this, and a little liquid starch added to the pigment will help, besides making it spread easier on the material. When ready mixed mediums are too thin, they may be left open to the air to thicken, or a little dry starch (cold water starch) may be added.

The common crayon is an excellent coloring medium and is discussed in this chapter under techniques. Felt-tip pens in various colors and sizes of tips are a must in any librarian's bag of tools.

Some coloring mediums are limited in their application to the library. Charcoal, pastels and colored chalk, while being easy to use and very effective, are so soft they will rub off on anything they contact unless sprayed with a fixative. A regular fixative may be used, but a cheap hair spray will do just as well. Inks applied with steel pens or brush are frequently used by the commercial artist, but many librarians may find they have little time for the practice required to become proficient with these tools, and their use more time consuming than some other method which would prove just as effective. Inks applied with a sponge or spreader, such as the Beta Inks, have some of the same failings, but they are easier to use and quite inexpensive.

Commercial letters and sign-making kits are available in a wide range of styles, sizes and colors from library, audio-visual and school supply houses and stationery stores. The most common of the commercial letters is probably the plastic letters with pin backs or re-usable adhesive. Unfortunately, these tend to be a bit expensive. Even so, every school should have at least one set of caps and lower case letters available to the staff. The librarian should select the style, color and mounting method which will allow for the greatest possible utility throughout the school system. Cardboard letters which may be pinned to the surface are inexpensive, and may be used as negative stencils as well. Contact letters, those you rub on, are excellent but usually too expensive for general use, though one use for them is suggested in the section of this chapter dealing with techniques.

Sign-making kits, such as the spray method used by the Jet-Ink Company, are good but limited to the sizes and styles of patterns that are available. These are probably more suitable for larger than normal letters, or where multiple copies are required.

A librarian may use carpet samples, construction paper, yarn, cloth, wallpaper or letters cut from brightly colored advertising. Whatever he uses, if it meets the criteria, it will be satisfactory.

Techniques

Newspaper mastheads, advertising copy, commercial posters, discarded alphabet books and graphic arts or typography titles containing alphabets are all sources for letters. These can be cut out and mounted to make a caption, used as patterns to be traced for cutting or painting or used as negative stencils when spray paints or inks are being used.

If the lettering is too small, it may be placed in the opaque projector, enlarged to the desired size and traced. This technique is often used when the typewriter is the source of letters. The caption is simply typed, the copy enlarged, traced and decorated. If the librarian has a typewriter with a multiple type head, it is easy to achieve a considerable variety in the style of letters using this technique.

Commercial letters with suitable mounting methods and pre-cut cardboard letters such as are often used by primary grade teachers, are quick and easy to use. There are many different styles and sizes, and unless a librarian has a variety, their constant use may result in the failure of the lettering to "fit" the design. Also, sameness in lettering might lead to boredom and so destroy some of the effectiveness of the bulletin board as a tool.

Contact letters are excellent for use with the Idea File. Though many of the cards in the file will be simply sketches and notes, many of them can be completed as bulletin boards in miniature to be placed in the opaque projector, enlarged and copied. When lettering the bulletin board in miniature, the contact letters need only be placed in position and rubbed with sufficient force to cause the inked surface to adhere to the card. These letters come in large sheets, in many different styles, sizes and colors.

Quick-Cut and Quick-Drawn Letters

There are a number of methods in use for making patterns for cut-out letters, or for drawing letters. While the suggestions offered here may not result in high-grade commercial quality, they will produce adequate letters, and do it quickly and quite simply.

Either the cut-out letters or the drawn letters utilize two basic designs, the cloud letters and block letters. Both are illustrated in complete alphabets at the conclusion of this chapter.

The quick-cut letters require only a pair of shears and the material to be used. The material is first cut into strips, each strip as wide as the intended height of the letters. If the librarian uses a paper cutter or exercises reasonable care in cutting, the strips do not need to be ruled out, and a few minutes time is saved. The strips are now placed together, one on top of the other, and pieces of nearly uniform size cut off. Each of these pieces should be the width of the letter. The "I" should be half of a piece, or somewhat less, while the "M" and "W" should be a bit wider since these letters are somewhat larger than the others. The result is a group of uniform patches of material, each one the size of the desired letters. With a little practice the librarian will be able to cut out the letters without first sketching them on the patches. If he doesn't have this much confidence, then the letter should be sketched, utilizing all of the patch, before cutting. Where two or more of the same letter are needed, a sufficient number of patches may be placed on top of one another, and all of them cut in one operation. This saves some time and helps insure a greater uniformity.

There may be some discrepancies in the uniformity of the letters, but they will prove so slight as not to detract from the appearance of the caption, or even be noticeable, when it is in place.

The material is first cut into strips, each strip
as wide as the intended height of the letters.

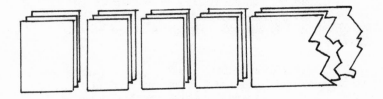

The strips are then cut into patches, each patch
as wide as the finished letter.

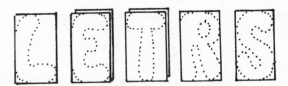

The patches are designed and cut out.   Note the
two E's and two T's are cut in one operation.

Block letters use exactly the same technique.   If the
librarian wishes to design the letters before cutting, he will
find it much simpler to first cut a tagboard template as wide
as the individual parts of the letters.   This template strip
may then be positioned and simply traced around to outline
the letter.   The template saves the time of measuring each
part of every letter with a ruler.

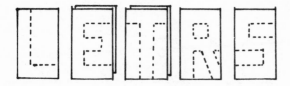

These letters use the same technique as the cloud letters.

In using the block letter design, it may occasionally be desirable to deliberately over-emphasize any lack of uniformity in the letters, thus producing a somewhat comic style of letters.   These, in exaggerated form, are often seen in the poster art that has become so popular.

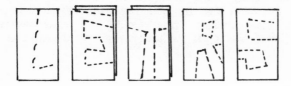

Quick-drawn letters use much the same technique as the cut-out letters except that top and bottom guidelines take the place of the paper strip.   The letters are drawn into the space the same as was done in placing the design on the patches for cutting out.   The spacing of letters is estimated and, with a reasonable amount of care, slight discrepancies in spacing will again not be noticeable.

Single line letters are the easiest to do and cloud letters are not difficult.   The block letters take a little more time.   Using a template as was done in designing the quick-cut letters, will save a considerable amount of time.   Block letters may also be done with a short piece of crayon or a wide-tipped fountain brush.   This technique is discussed later in the chapter.

Single Line   Cloud Letters   Block Letters
Letters

With a little practice, a quicker method may be used in drawing letters. The method requires only a yardstick or other straightedge. No top line is needed, for with a little practice the librarian can judge the height as well as the spacing of the letters with sufficient accuracy by eye.

The straightedge is placed on the surface and each letter is drawn so that its base rests against, and is squared off by the straightedge. This results in a neat, square edge along the bottoms of all the letters, giving the illusion of carefully drafted lettering.

There are several excellent mediums for drawing letters, and the librarian may like to experiment with some of them.

The common crayon is one of the most versatile of tools. Block letters may be easily done by simply breaking off a piece of crayon as long as the width of each part of the letter. Holding the crayon with its side resting on the surface, it is dragged across the paper, making a line as wide as the crayon is long. A kind of Barnum Type may be created by the same technique except that the crayon is kept at all times in a horizontal position. This creates a letter of mixed wide and thin lines, all horizontal lines being wide, and all verticals being narrow. An interesting shading effect can be produced with the first crayon technique except the crayon is held on the end that makes the outside perimeter of the letters. The outside edges of the letters will be dark, and the lines fading out to nothing along the interior edges. The effect is more dainty and feminine than the bold solid colors. These techniques are mentioned in connection with the block letters, but they can be used to form the single line letters as well.

Two crayons, pencils or felt-tip pens may be fastened together with a rubber band and used as one drawing instrument. This technique will require a bit of practice but some interesting and varied letter styles may be quickly and easily created.

Use your fingers and finger paint to produce letters if you don't mind the mess. If you don't like the feel of finger paint try a bit of sponge instead of your finger. The children will like the results. The sponge can also be used for a stippled effect. The lighter the pressure on the sponge, the less color and the more open the stippling.

The quickest and easiest lettering tool to use is probably the felt-tip pen. These come in many colors and in a range of sizes of tips. If the oil-base ink type, the so-called permanent ink, is used, the pen will write on almost any type of surface.

The quick-cut letters are very easy to do in 3-D. Two sheets of material of contrasting or complementary colors are used. These are placed back to back, and, with care so as not to move them, the materials are cut into strips, and then into patches. The letters are cut from the patches, being very careful not to let the two pieces of material slip while cutting. When the letters are cut out, the bottom color is pushed up, or down and to the side. This gives the illusion of depth to the letter. These may then be cemented together, or simply pinned to the surface, the pins holding them in place.

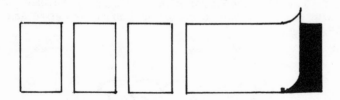

The strips and patches are first cut.

The letters are cut from the patches.

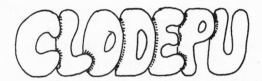

Here the bottom letter was moved up and to the right.

The "cloud" letters may be placed as single letters as has been previously illustrated, or overlapped to form a cloud.   These are fun to make and are especially adaptable to comic themes and the cartoon type designs.

Either cut or drawn letters may be used, but they are so placed that each letter slightly overlaps the one following.   The overlapping parts may be slightly outlined with a felt-tip pen or crayon to make them more definitive and easier to read.

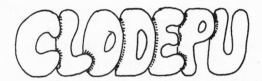

Psychedelic captions may be made several ways, but one of the easiest is to place the caption on a sheet of construction paper, and trim, leaving a margin around the let-

Pen and ink or brush techniques are very old, very
effective, and in common artistic use, but probably few librarians will find the time for sufficient practice to become
adequately proficient with them.   Perhaps the easiest to use,
and the librarian might consider it, is the Beta Ink technique.
This uses a fast-drying ink in several colors, and a sponge
in different widths as the spreader.   Though a little practice
is necessary to use this medium effectively, it is not as
difficult as pen and ink or brush techniques.

There are several common types of stencils ranging
from the cheap cardboard or ruler stencil found in most
school kids' desks to outfits like the LeRoy Lettering Kits.
Though adequate lettering can be achieved with their use,
the stencil can be time consuming, and surprisingly difficult
in spacing and maintaining even lines.   The author has no
quarrel with them, and they are frequently used, but in the
search for time-saving methods of forming captions on bulletin boards, they would be one of the final choices.

Hand print sets are available in most schools, and
they are an excellent teaching medium with youngsters, but
they are most difficult for the librarian's lettering needs.
It is difficult to line up the letters, the density of the ink
tends to vary quite a bit and a good printing job simply takes
too much time.   Then too, the librarian is limited in style
and size to the sets available for his use.

Many school systems have sign-making outfits of one
kind or another, most of them consisting of a mounting
surface and letters to be slipped into place.   These are excellent for posting the menu in the cafeteria, announcing the
date and time of the next home game, or making some other
announcement.   Few of them have little value to the librarian in bulletin board construction.

One librarian suggested cutting letters from potatoes
and using these letters to print the captions.   This is a
"fun" art activity for the classroom, but it would appear
that the time spent cutting the letters from potatoes could
be of more value spent in reading guidance, selection, or
even just relaxing.

The ultimate solution to the problems of lettering
the bulletin board, and bulletin board execution itself, lies
in the employment of a professional graphic artist.   Few li-
braries could afford this service.   The services of the

ters. This is then cemented to another color con
paper, and trimmed again. The process may be c
until the desired effect is achieved.

The psychedelic designs may appear as something of
a mess to many of us, but young patrons consider such designs "in" and the wise librarian will occasionally use them.

Spray methods, using stencils, are sometimes useful.
The Jet-Inks are especially good where captions need to be
duplicated or are required in larger than normal sizes. The
process uses plastic foam letters which are positioned on
the paper. A screen is then placed over the letters, and
the surface sprayed with the ink. If several copies are
needed, the ink is allowed to dry so that the letters will adhere to the screen. Slipping another sheet of paper under
the screen is all that is required to duplicate the caption.
A number of interesting techniques are described in the literature accompanying the Jet-Ink sets.

Letters cut from advertising and other sources or
the commercial cardboard letters may be used in much the
same way. These are positioned on the surface and, using
care not to blow them out of position, or holding them in
place with a bit of photographer's wax or rubber cement, the
area around them is sprayed with paint. When the paint is
dry, the patterns are removed and may be stored for future
use.

Spray techniques do have library application, but they
are a bit messy, they do take some time, and they are
limited to the style of letters available for stencil use.

Some common lettering techniques are not highly
recommended for general library use because of time in-
volved, or difficulty in handling.

school art department, artistic students or talented individuals among the friends of the library might be available if the librarian took the time to seek them out. When using such resource people the librarian should choose the design and theme, for the bulletin board must remain a professional tool of the library, used to help solve those professional problems where its use might be indicated.

Sources for Commercial Letters

The following list of sources for commercial letters and supplies is not complete nor is it given here with any special recommendations. The suppliers are those with which the author is familiar or those recommended by other librarians. Prices are not included because of frequent change.

Nasco   Fort Atkinson, Wis.   53538
Nasco West   Box 3837, Modesto, Cal.   95352
Cut-out letters from 90-point board in sets of 150 or 350 letters. These range in size from 3/4 to 4-1/2 inches high and are made up in black, red, blue, white, gold and silver. These letters may be mounted with pins or adhesive and are re-usable. Nasco also has a good line of stencils and templates if the librarian is interested.

Stick-A-Letter, Visual Letters   Rt. 6, Box 1400, Escondido, Cal.   92025
These letters are stamped from construction paper, or from six-ply cardboard. The paper letters are made in ten different colors, and the cardboard ones come in red, black and white. These range from 2 to 4 inches high, mount by contact, and are re-usable several times. (When the contact cement is no longer usable a bit of photographer's wax or Stik-Taks may be used.)

Cello-Tak Mfg., Inc.   35 Alabama Ave., Island Park, Long Island, New York
These are dry transfer alphabets that are applied simply by rubbing the letter after it has been positioned. They come in sheets in a number of styles and sizes and are obtainable in most stationery stores.

Judy Alphabets, any supply house.
These letters are stamped from heavy white stock and range from 1-1/4 to 3 inches high. Though these are

designed for use on flannel boards, they can be mounted
with pins, photographer's wax or Stik-Taks.

American Instructional Materials, Inc.   Box 22748, Texas
    Women's University Station, Denton, Texas   76204
        This company produces a good plastic pin back letter
in a modern gothic style in black or white and either 1-1/4
or 2 inches high.

American Seating   Box 24148, San Francisco, Cal.   94124
        A somewhat cheaper pin back plastic letter is offered
in white and a range in size from 1 to 3 inches in height.

Construction Playthings   1040 East 85th St., Kansas City,
    Mo. 64131
        Their natural finish plywood letters come in 3-1/2
inch caps and 2-1/4 inch lower case.   These need mounting
holes drilled in them.

American Jet Spray Industries, Inc.   1240 Harlan Street,
    Denver, Col.
        The Jet-Ink Sign Making Kit uses a negative stencil
or pattern and a screen to hold the patterns in place.   The
ink is then sprayed onto the surface.   These kits are especially adaptable to large letters and where duplicate captions are needed.

ABCDEFGHIJ
KLMNOPQRS
TUVWXYZ
abcdefghijklm
nopqrstuvwxy
z

ABCDEFGHIJ
KLMNOPQRS
TUVWXYZ

abcdefghijklmnopqrst
uvwxyz

Part II

DESIGN IDEAS

Suggested Designs

Chapter 4

QUICK DESIGNS FOR THE BUSY LIBRARIAN

These suggested designs should probably be called simply "Quickies," because that is just what they are. There are times when a librarian is just too busy with other chores, and there is little time to devote to design construction. That is when these designs prove helpful, for they can all be done in a very short time, many of them by one of the young student librarians.

Three quickly con-
structed bulletin boards are
illustrated here. The space
is first covered with colored
construction paper, craft paper or, perhaps, a piece of
fabric. A contrasting color
is added as an attractor. This
may be either a rectangular
shape, cut into a free form,
or suggestive of some object
such as the grass illustrated
here.

Added interest may be
gained by raising the overlay on
small blocks. This creates a
shadow which gives dimension
to the space.

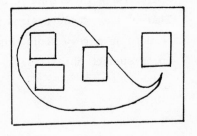

This type of design is
very effective in a hallway or
along any blank wall where
there is no bulletin board
mounting surface provided. It
can also be made free standing
for use in a hall or a display
window.

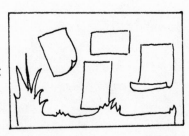

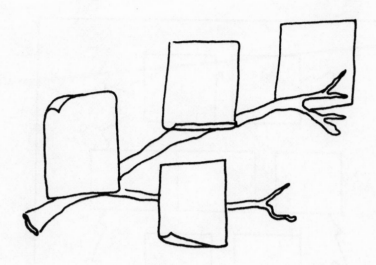

      This is a very quick and simple display. An inter-
esting branch or light piece of driftwood provides the attractor. This particular display used a piece of manzanita
mounted on a pink background. No caption was used, but
one could be added if the librarian felt the need.

      These bits of interesting wood are nice to use on a
counter display, or, if smaller pieces are used, they work
well into smaller poster designs. Collecting them can also
be a rewarding experience if you enjoy a stroll through
woods or along beaches.

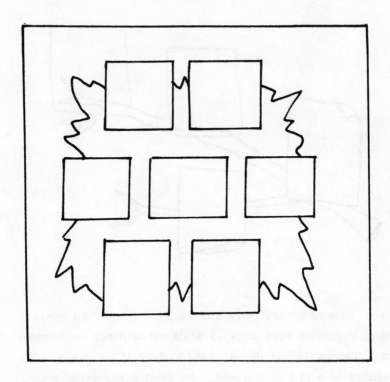

A sheet of red metallic wrapping paper was first
mounted to the space. Black construction paper with torn edges
was mounted over this, and the book jackets added.

Most any type of contrasting materials could be used in
this design, but it is more effective if different type materials are also used, such as a piece of brightly printed
fabric with an overlay of construction paper.

A caption should not be used, for it would detract from
the overall design which is very overpowering by itself.

This quick board used much the same technique as the one on the preceding page, except that the overlay has the openings torn into it, and rolled back to make something of a frame for the book jackets which are mounted on the background surface.

Any contrasting or complementary colors may be used.

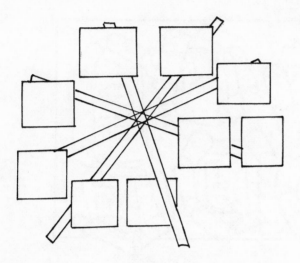

This design may not appear to amount to much, but children like it and, probably because of its simplicity, will borrow it for their own poster and design work. The "rods" were cut from various colored papers and mounted on a light gray background. The book jackets were somewhat staggered around the outside edges.

This design also works well on a bare wall, or as a simple poster design with a single book jacket or message added to just one of the rods.

This type of design should not be centered in the space it will occupy or it becomes too geometric and formal.

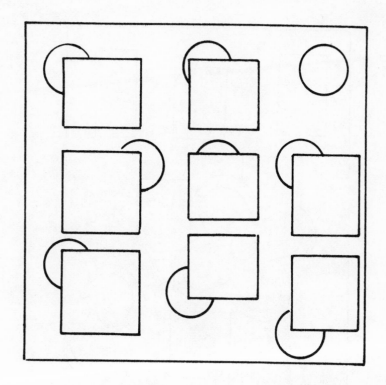

Paper disks may be cut from any kind of paper or cardboard that happens to be handy. The colors may reflect a seasonal motif, or a particular holiday, such as orange and black for Halloween.

Though the book jacket arrangement is geometric, the placement of the disks helps to break up the straight lines.

A neutral background color must be used with this type of display, especially when different colors are used for the disks.

The large flowers were cut from blue and white construction paper. The blue paper was cut larger than the white
to form the outer edge. The white paper was then cemented
only near the center of the blue so that it would be a bit
floppy. A yellow center was added and a wide green stem.

These and the book jackets were mounted on a pink
background.

What this design lacks in originality, it makes up for in color, for it uses a lot of it. The space is first covered with a neutral color. Each of the strips of paper are a different color, and, of course, the lettering is different colors too. All the other lettering should be black or white or the design will lose all continuity.

This board is in a way a teaching board, or more of a testing board, because it suggests no titles but forces the patron to go to the 300 shelf to search, or to the card catalog to locate the desired materials.

When a staff member asks for an art idea, the librarian is presented with a perfect opportunity to circulate these titles, for children love to draw these figures, and several objectives may be achieved at one time.

Chapter 5

STREAMER TYPE DISPLAYS

Occasionally there is need for a long streamer type display, such as might be used along a blank wall to tie together the various displays being used at a book fair, or simply as a decorative device in a hallway or the cafeteria.

The following suggestions have all been used, and were selected for inclusion because of their success, economy of time and material, and ease of construction.

The little engine and cars are easily cut from construction paper. When mounted to a wall, loaded with book
jackets, a very decorative streamer display is created. This
one also looks good when mounted along the top of shelving
or along a counter.

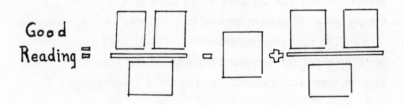

This is another quick and easy streamer display design. The math symbols are cut from colored construction
paper and mounted to a wall along with the book jackets. Of
course, other math symbols could also be used.

This design is most effective when used with older
children or materials related to the upper grades.

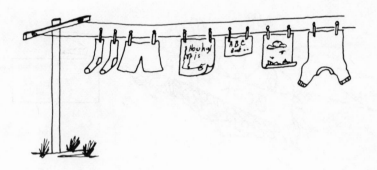

This design shows only one half of a long streamer
type display. The clothesline poles were cut from cardboard,
painted with aluminum paint, and fastened to the wall with photographer's wax. The long clothesline was heavy white yarn
which was kept from too much sagging by the application of occasional bits of photographer's wax along its lengths. Book jackets, some of them lightly curved, were "hung" on the line along
with clothing cut from construction paper. The clothespins were
glued to the items hung on the line, and then attached to the wall
with bits of photographer's wax.

The ground line under the poles was cut from green
construction paper.

This design has been used to help tie together the
various book exhibits at book fairs as well as an occasional
decoration.

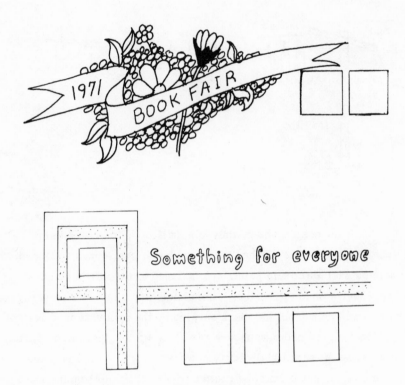

The top streamer display was simply placed under the opaque projector, enlarged to size and traced. The small background flowers were then painted purple, the others yellow and red, and the leaves green. The banner was left white and lettered with a black felt-tip pen.

The second display used long lengths of craft paper on which a thinner strip of decorative wrapping paper had been glued. The streamer might run the entire length of the display, or two might be used mounted on either end and extending only a short way toward the center. Both methods have been used with equal effectiveness.

Gray construction paper boards make up this fence which was mounted on the wall and book jackets and posters arranged to complete the display.

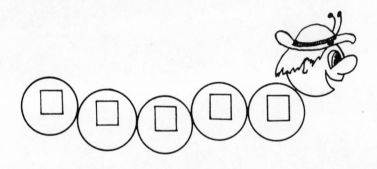

Rounds of construction paper, each with a book jacket make up this worm. He can be as long as you like, or you might want to use two or three, depending upon the length of your space. This is one of the quickest streamer displays to construct.

Chapter 6

GENERAL PURPOSE DISPLAY

The designs in this section are of a general nature. Many of them could be used in a special area, but most of them are simply attractors to be used with titles and materials covering a wide variety of subjects.

I don't know exactly where I got the idea for this display, but everyone liked it. I covered the space with black paper, and used crayons on a white sheet to make my drawing of a girl reading a book. The balloon was put on white paper, colored with crayon and mounted on another sheet of black paper. The round dots used to point out the balloon were cut from black paper. Book jackets were arranged in the space, and some of my favorite titles were set on the top of the book case.

The design was easy to build, but I had to keep putting other titles on the book case as the kids checked them out.

Debbie Fiora
5th Grade
East Lake School

    This design has been used to advertise books on history, government and general themes.

    The hat and coat were cut from black paper, the face from pinkish-tan, and the hair white. The ruff was added last and was cut from paper doilies and lightly sculptured before cementing in place. The bell was cut from gold foil paper, and the handle added with a brown crayon. The caption was also printed with a brown crayon.

    The entire design was mounted on a light gray surface.

    This design could also be done as a cartoon.

Mounted on a white background these green construction paper plants with their book jacket flowers make an attractive display, and a very easy and quick one to construct.
The caption was added with a black felt-tip pen.

Look what's Cookin'!

This upper-grade design is a simple black on white cartoon. The little cook was traced onto the surface, painted with black paint, and the book jackets added.

He could be done in as much detail and as much color as time will allow, even to giving him a cloth apron and gloves. However, the cartoon technique is just about as effective, and much less time consuming to construct.

The metallic green fish with black contruction lines
are swimming across a background of light yellow-green paper. The book jackets are slightly curled. No caption is
needed with this board.

An interesting variation is to cut the fish from cellophane. The change in color where they overlap creates an
interesting effect. The design is aided by a background of
yellow-green rainbow effect tissue paper.

These fish can also be built from aluminum pie plates
or cut from printed fabric or pages from a wallpaper sample
book.

The octopus was cut from black construction paper with the white areas cut from white paper and cemented in place. The design was then mounted to a very light green background and the book jackets added.

No caption was added, but one could be inserted in the upper right-hand portion of the board above the octopus.

The bookworm on a green paper leaf is simply an attractor. This one has been done on heavy green tagboard and is a part of the library's circulating collection of display materials.

Though this worm was cut from cotton fabric that had a tiny floral design and the black bands were colored with a felt-tip pen, it might be constructed from most anything.

The worm was raised from the leaf about half an inch by the use of blocks. The leaf was also raised from the space by about the same distance. This gives some dimension to the design and added interest.

This design was done as a simple black on white cartoon. The only color was provided by the book covers, which were lightly shaded with crayon. This design can be quickly completed by simply placing the design in the opaque projector, enlarging it to size, and tracing with a felt-tip pen. Coloring takes only a few seconds.

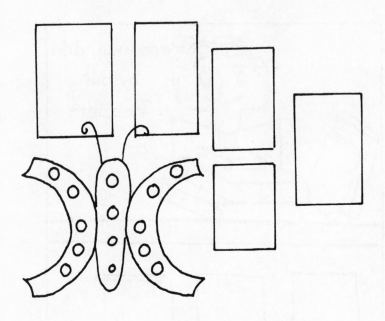

The simple butterfly design is shown here simply
as an attractor to a general display, though the design could
be used to advertise titles on insects or even spring.

The design can be cut from most any type of material that is brightly colored and quite flashy, then mounted
over a harmonious or contrasting color.

The butterfly may be mounted directly to the space,
but its attractiveness is enhanced by raising him from the
surface on small blocks.

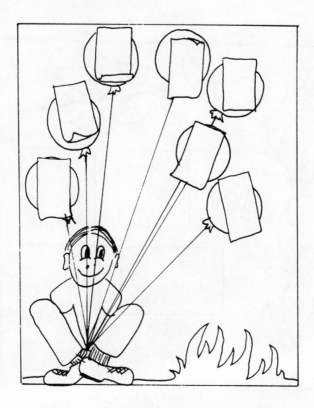

This is one of those designs which may not appear
to be of much use for anything, and yet, it proves successful as an attractor.

The space was covered with blue paper, and the
green grass and ground line were added. The figure was
simply traced over the background with a black felt-tip pen.
Circles of different colors were cut and mounted to the
space with lengths of string running from each one to the
point in the design where they were being held. The book
jackets, some slightly curled, were added last.

No caption is needed with this design, though one
could be added if it was felt necessary. Though this design
was used simply as a general interest theme, it could direct
attention to book selection in any area of the library simply by
selecting the proper book jackets for display.

    This design used sprigs of plastic greenery and flowers for the design, but these could be cut from paper, painted, or be paper artificials. Many craft books give directions for making these.

    This makes a quick seasonal board as well as a decorative one. For fall, substitute fall colors for the leaves and bunches of berries for the flowers.

    This design is more attractive with older students, and is an excellent attractor for use in the professional library, or with poster work.

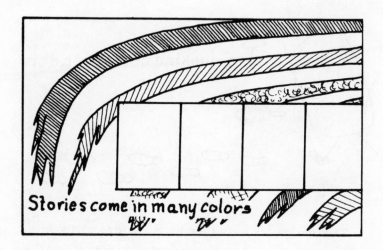

The color bands may be painted on a white surface
and allowed to run a bit, or they may be cut from colored
papers and cemented in place.

This design was developed by a fifth-grade student
from a poster she had made to help illustrate a book she
was reporting on to her class.

The caption was added with a brush and black tempera
paint.

This design for a smaller board is pure cartoon.
The body of the figure is a book jacket. Though it is trite
and very common, it is used from time to time, both as a
bulletin board and as a poster, and always is a success.

Children often use this for bake sales, but with the
substitution of a cupcake or a cookie for the book jacket,
and a change in the caption to I'm looking for an eater ...
or a buyer.

Though this design is suggested for a streamer display, with the "bugs" scattered, it can also be used for a bulletin board.

These "bugs" were simply enlarged to size, traced in outline, and cut from construction paper. The long legs were pipe cleaners cemented in place and body lines were added with a black felt-tip pen.

Greater detail may be used if the time is available to construct them. Wings may be made a different color than the body and cemented in place, or they can be partially sculptured. Artistic students could put them together in many different ways.

This friendly little bookworm might be used to provide an attractor to just about any subject the librarian might choose.

He may be completed as a simple inked cartoon, or be painted in any color desired, or cut from any decorative material.

East Lake School has one cut from heavy cardboard and painted light green with bright yellow markings. He circulates throughout the school and, even under fairly heavy use, does not appear to loose his attractiveness to the children.

READING FOR RAINY DAYS

This design was painted onto a sheet of tagboard and then cut out before mounting over a light blue surface.

Almost any colors can be used so long as they are not drab.

The raindrops were cut from scraps of white paper and pinned in place.

This design can easily be changed to a winter scene by removing the umbrella, and substituting tiny snowflakes for the raindrops.

This is a very simple and effective design, and needs no caption. It lends itself to just about any medium of decoration or construction the librarian might choose.

The most effective appears to be cut paper. The background is first covered with a warm, medium-dark color. The faces are then cut from a contrasting, lighter-tone paper. Hair is cut from any other color that will contrast with the faces and the background, and cemented in place. Facial features are added with felt-tip pens or paints, and the completed cut-outs mounted to the surface.

This design preserves the borders of the bulletin board space, but the faces could be done fully round and mounted partly beyond the edge to break up the geometric border effect, if desired.

If a caption is used, it should be added to the top of the space.

The wings of these butterflies were cut from green foil wrapping paper. The bodies and heads were yellow construction paper with black bands and faces. Antennae were white pipe cleaners cemented to the back of the head. The decorative dots were cut from bits of pink fabric and cemented into place.

The book jackets were first mounted on the pale pink surface and the butterflies were added last. No caption was used, for the board offered books of a general nature.

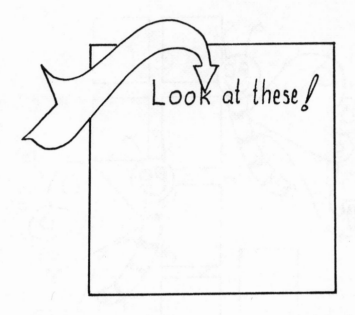

This is a very simple design and takes only a minute to construct.

After the space had been covered with a warm pastel color, the arrow was cut from a piece of complementary printed fabric and mounted in the space. The caption was done with a wide felt-tip pen in black. The addition of book jackets completed the design.

This design has been used for new books as well as older titles that needed advertising. The figures were cut from flesh-colored paper, with hair, cut from yellow or brown paper, cemented in place; facial features were added last with a felt-tip pen.

The space was first covered with a dark green paper. Heavy white yarn was then pinned in place and the figures added. "LOOK" was cut from white construction paper and the rest of the caption lettered with a water color brush and thick white poster paint. Book jackets were added last to complete the display.

One librarian used actual photographs of some of the students in place of the paper figures and changed the caption to "Look what we found." She reported that the kids had a lot of fun with this, and they did charge out quite a few of the titles.

A white sky and blue water make up the background for this display. The book jackets were pinned in place and a bit of netting was pinned over them. The fish were cut from green metallic wrapping paper and a black felt-tip pen used to outline the eye, gills and lateral line. The boat was cut from red construction paper, while the oar and fisherman were colored in with a black felt-tip pen. The lettering was done with a red felt-tip pen.

This design is very easy to do, and takes only a few minutes. If the library does not have a piece of netting to use, chicken wire will do just as well.

The danger to a design of this nature is over-decoration. Some librarians want to add star fish, sea horses, fish net floats and seaweed, but this only results in decorative clutter which detracts from the book jackets which are the principal purpose of the display.

I tried an experiment with my design. Instead of simply drawing a girl, I made a longer, more narrow board, and brought her dress around in a curve to help keep sight lines in the space. I didn't quite succeed with this, but the board was bright and the titles I suggested received good circulation.

The design and caption I cut from construction paper and mounted on a dark brown surface. I lightly sculptured the hair and dress to give it more shape.

Teri Dringenberg
5th Grade
East Lake School

Chapter 7

DISPLAYS FOR NEW ACQUISITIONS

Many librarians keep a shelf, or an area in the library available for new acquisitions where they can be displayed, and are easy for the patrons of the library to locate and to browse. This is generally sufficient when only a few new titles are being added at a time.

When a number of titles are added, as is often done in the fall and spring, a display drawing attention to the new titles is often desirable.

Though there are many possible designs suggesting new materials, the following have proven to be the most attractive and the easiest to construct.

YOUR NEW BOOKS, MASTER

The space was first covered with black paper. The gray "smoke" from the lamp was added over this. The Genie was cut from white paper with the shaded portions colored green. The head and arms were outlined with black felt-tip pen. The head scarf was lightly colored with a red crayon and the jewel was an old plastic ornament cemented in place. Face and arms were lightly colored with an orange crayon. The lamp was cut from gold wrapping paper. The caption was lettered in with a fine brush and aluminum paint. The book jackets were lightly curled before mounting.

This design takes a bit longer to construct than some of the others, but its success makes the added time worth the effort.

Come the
New Books

This cartoon design was developed by an eighth-grade boy and was intended to poke a little fun at his teacher.

The design was placed in the opaque projector and simply drawn onto a white surface with a black felt-tip pen. The book jackets were trimmed and added to the box. The cart wheel was cut from red paper and added for a spot of color.

For a long time "Mr. Dupe" as the kids called him (no reference to the teacher) appeared on posters selling goodies, tickets to games, concerts and plays, making announcements and carrying the current lunch menu as well as being used in the library.

Though this illustration was used to advertise new
books, the subject is equally suitable for spring or Easter.

The little chick was cut from yellow construction paper. A real white bow was added along with a bonnet cut
from white fabric. The caption was cut from white construction paper. The entire design was mounted over a black
surface.

This design has never been used as a cartoon, but it
would probably be quite effective done this way for upper
grades.

This figure was first cut from a light salmon-colored paper. The skirt and blouse were cut from fabric scraps and cemented in place. The hair was painted yellow with tempera paint, and the shoes black.

The dog was cut from white paper, and the spots painted brown. The caption was lettered in brown on a strip of white paper.

The design and book jackets were mounted on a light green surface.

The little chick is usable for spring, Easter, new materials, or a simple decoration for an attractor.

The little chick was cut from yellow paper, and the eggshell from white. The shaded portion of the eggshell was added with a black felt-tip pen. The eyes, the beak and other lines were also done with a black felt-tip pen. The grass and ground-line were cut from green construction paper.

The completed design was mounted on a beige background.

This design has also been done as a cartoon black on white, and used successfully with upper-grade children and in the professional library.

Chapter 8

SPECIAL SUBJECTS

There are many occasions for displays relating to some special subject area of the curriculum. This is also an area the librarian may find need for permanent-type displays that can be charged out by teachers in the various grades and departments for their own class room and departmental use.

These suggested designs may be used by the librarian in any way that will best suit his purposes.

A length of cord and large fish hooks were used in this display, because the spool of film and the study print case were items of realia. The fish was cut from pink paper with black construction lines added with a crayon. The display was mounted over a light blue background, and the caption was added with a black felt-tip pen.

This type of design would not be usable in a library with closed A.V. shelves, for there would be no purpose for it. Where A.V. material is made available to the young patrons, an occasional advertising of these materials may be desirable.

This design has been used both as a poster and as a bulletin board in the reference section of the library.

Both fish and worm were cut from metallic foil wrapping paper, the fish in green and the worm in red. A black felt-tip pen was used to make the markings. The worm was strung on a paper fish hook attached to a length of white yarn. Both fish and worm were mounted on small blocks to raise them from the surface a bit.

The caption was placed on the light blue background with a red felt-tip pen.

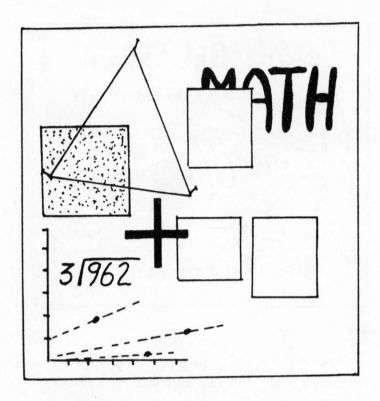

    The square, addition sign and caption were cut from
construction paper and mounted to a white surface. The
triangle was made from yarn pinned to the surface. Every-
thing else was inked in with a black felt-tip pen.

    Similar simple designs using the symbols from chem-
istry, physics or other areas of the curriculum may also be
used.

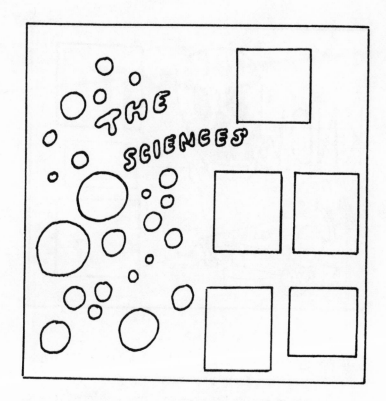

The bubbles were cut from light-colored construction paper and metallic foil wrapping paper mounted on a black background.   The caption was painted in with aluminum paint, and the book jackets added.

One librarian tried this design using balloons, but the children associated balloons with parties rather than the sciences, and the design didn't prove effective.   The bubbles don't represent anything in particular, but at least they do not suggest something other than that intended, and so prove to be effective attractors.

The cigarette, capsule, pill and parts of the hypodermic needle were cut from construction paper. The skull was cut from white paper and the shaded areas painted in with black paint. The skull was mounted on blocks to raise it a bit from the board. The smoke was gray yarn allowed to sag loosely. The completed design was mounted over dark green paper.

This type of design is often ineffective in aiding circulation of materials on this topic, not so much from a fault of the design, as of the type of material itself. Often young people seem to be embarrassed by it. Still, the material needs to be advertised, and displays seem to be about as effective as other methods that have been tried.

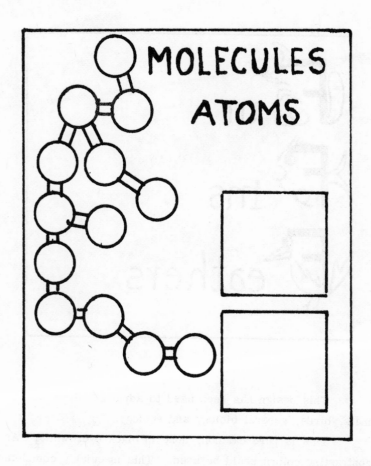

This molecular chain was constructed from various colors of construction paper with yellow rods connecting the atoms. These and the book jackets were mounted on a dark purple surface, and the caption was painted on with thick white tempera paint and a watercolor brush.

This design has been used to advertise titles on animals, birds, general biology and ecology.

This is pure cartoon, done in black over white. Any contrasting colors could be used. This is quickly completed by placing the design in the opaque projector, enlarging to size and simply tracing.

The addition of book jackets completes the display.

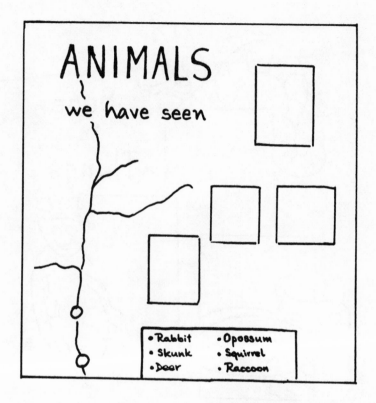

This is something of an "add-on" design as it grows
during the time it is maintained. The design consists of a
background in a light color on which a map of the immediate
school-home area has been drawn. As the children report
seeing different animals, they are added to the legend, and
the proper marking noted on the map at the location of the
sighting.

The activity not only draws attention to the book jackets, which are changed from time to time, but helps children
become more aware of the things around them, and younger
children to identify some of the animals they see.

This design is more suitable for a rural area such
as ours, but even in a city, there are birds, and sometimes
a surprising array of animals too.

These bugs were cut from different colored foil wrapping paper by a sixth-grade boy who designed them. The legs and other necessary additions were done with a black felt-tip pen.

The bugs were mounted over a light gray background, and the caption was added with a felt-tip pen.

This design was selected as a winner in the library's annual "Design a Bulletin Board" contest.

This simple design was cut from construction paper and mounted on a light blue background. The cloud was cut from white paper with construction lines added with a gray felt-tip pen. The yellow sun had construction lines in black. The yellow bolt of lightning added balance to the design. The caption was lettered with a black felt-tip pen.

The background for this design was white paper. The tree trunk was cut from brown construction paper and the bark lines were added with a black felt-tip pen. The trunk was added to the surface, and the green paper tree top was added along with the green ground line. Book jackets were curled as illustrated before mounting to the surface, and the caption was added with a brown felt-tip pen.

This is another design that is easily adaptable to a blank wall, or to a free-standing design.

This design is shown here as a poster, but it has also been used as a bulletin board with the book jackets arranged around the picture as a framing device.

This isn't as difficult as it looks, though it does take a few minutes to complete. The design is first enlarged to size and traced onto the space. It is then painted with black tempera paint. If desired, the captions can be lettered on other paper and pinned to the completed drawing.

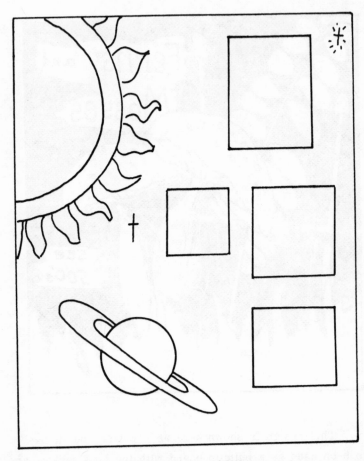

Space and astronomy are the dual themes of this larger board. The design is built on a deep blue background. The inner part of the sun is white paper, the outer rim is yellow, and the rays are orange. The planet was cut from light blue paper with a white paper ring. The two little star-like figures were done with a watercolor brush and a bit of aluminum paint.

The design was very striking and proved to be a powerful attractor.

This board was a simple black on white cartoon.
Though no book jackets are shown, in use they were lightly
curled and scattered at random in the space.

There is no reason why this design couldn't be done
in color. It has always worked quite well as a cartoon, so
the time was never taken to complete it in any other medium.

This very simple board was painted onto a beige-colored surface with green tempera paint. This design shows only two book jackets, but more could be added along each side if desired.

This design is not pretty, in fact, it actually repels. But its attracting quality lies in the fact that it is not pretty, and the topic it "sells" is timely.

The water shapes in this design were cut from light blue paper. The reeds were cut from green and the cattails were painted brown with a felt-tip marking pen. The birds were cut from white paper. The design was mounted on a purple background, with the caption done in black with a felt-tip pen.

This board was used successfully with older children, and in the science department and professional library.

The space was first covered with a light blue paper. The water lines were cut from darker blue and added next. The green rushes were cut from paper, and the cattails cemented to the back before mounting.

The duck was cut from brown paper and added along with the book jackets. The caption was added with a red felt-tip pen.

This display could also be used for conservation, ecology or related areas.

These designs illustrate the use of a motif of a given subject, and are easy to construct. The parts are simply cut from construction paper of suitable color and mounted over a white, or contrasting colored surface. The captions are either lettered in, or done effectively with pin-back lettering.

These designs are also suitable for poster work.

This killer whale doesn't look much like a killer as he romps among the book jackets against a pale blue background.

The figure was cut from black and white construction paper with a blue eye added for a spot of color. The caption was inked onto the background with a black felt-tip pen.

After the book jackets were in place, the whale was mounted, being raised from the surface about two inches. Two-inch strips of cardboard tubing were used for blocks.

This simple design was done in cartoon style with a black felt-tip pen on light blue paper. The only color was the whale which was cut from purple paper with a white paper "blow." This was done to give a central point of interest to the design to focus attention.

The design has been painted in colors, but it proved just as effective as a cartoon, and this technique took less time.

This design was built very much the same way as the preceding one. The water was cut from blue paper, the weeds and tree tops from green, and the tree trunks from brown. The lettering was done with a brown felt-tip pen on a background of white paper that had been used to first cover the mounting surface

When used without background, this design can also be used on a blank wall.

The space was first covered with a light blue paper
to suggest sky. The white paper clouds, with added detail
lines in black, were added next. The birds were cut from
construction paper, and the top part of their wings colored
black. These were pinned in place only at the center to allow the wings to stand out from the space. The bird in the
background was put in with a black felt-tip pen, as was the
caption. The book jackets were lightly curled before mounting.

The design may be used with weather, atmosphere or
any other suggested subject.

This little board was used to advertise only two titles, but the cat could be elongated to span more titles, or easily be stood on a block arrangement.

The body of the cat was cut from light brown construction paper and mounted to the white surface. The head was cut from the same construction paper, the green eyes, black nose and mouth added with felt-tip pens, and then mounted on small blocks to raise it from the surface of the board and give it more form.

The design could be used to advertise other areas of the collection than cats.

"Fido" is best done as a line-drawing cartoon, either in a simple black on white, using a felt-tip pen or black crayon for lining, or, where color is desired, the surface may be first covered and the drawing done with a contrasting felt-tip pen or fine brush and fairly thick tempera or poster paint.

This design suggests titles about dogs because of the caption, but the design is effective when used simply as a decorative attractor for titles on most any subject.

The children have frequently borrowed this design for poster work advertising sales and events.

An interesting method of construction may be achieved by tracing the design onto a sheet of paper and cutting it out. The nose and mouth area is then cut out and when the design is mounted to the surface, this area is raised on blocks to give some shape to the figure.

The same basic design is again used here, except the position of the hind leg is changed, and motion lines are added.   Otherwise it is completed the same as his twin on the preceding page.

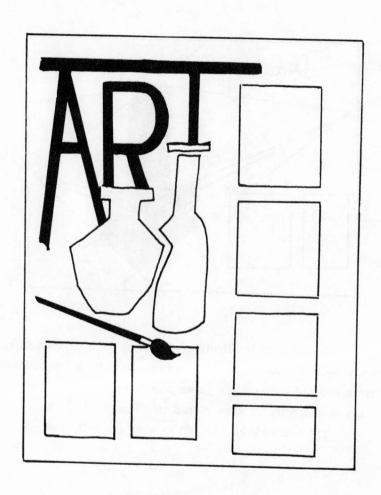

Any colors of construction paper may be used to cut the various objects used as attractors as well as the caption. When ready for mounting, the board should be covered with a contrasting paper that will show up the objects.

Though this board is very formal, it has proven quite effective.

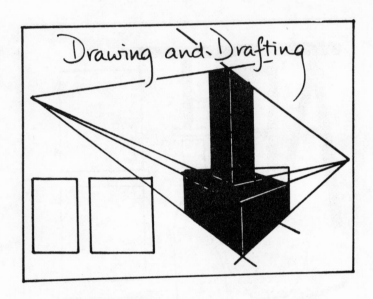

This design is effective when done as a cartoon black on white. It has also been completed by cutting the building from colored construction paper and adding the construction lines with lengths of yarn pinned in place.

The caption was lettered in with a felt-tip pen.

This little figure may be done in color, but it is much simpler and just as effective to enlarge to desired size and trace with a black felt-tip pen.

Here the design has been used to "sell" materials dealing with photography, but it can also be used with conservation and birds. The bird, of course, could be changed to anything else the librarian might desire.

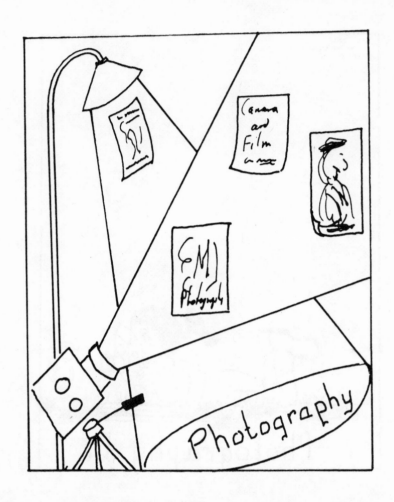

The background for this board was black. The fixtures were cut from white paper, and the light beams were cut from yellow and mounted to the surface. The addition of book jackets and the black caption completed the design.

This one is very easy to do, and requires only a very few minutes to complete.

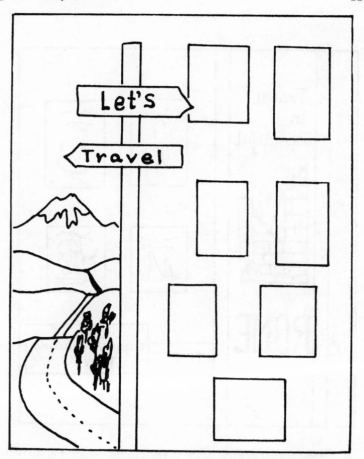

The surface was first covered with white craft paper. The picture side was painted on, starting first with a patch of blue sky extending nearly to the top of the space. The snow was left unpainted, while the distant mountain was colored purple. The far hills were colored dark green, the closer ones light green and the foreground yellow. The road was left white.

The sign post and signs were cut from light brown paper with the caption added with thick white paint.

The design boosted the circulation of travel books, and kept the circulation high for quite a while after it was removed.

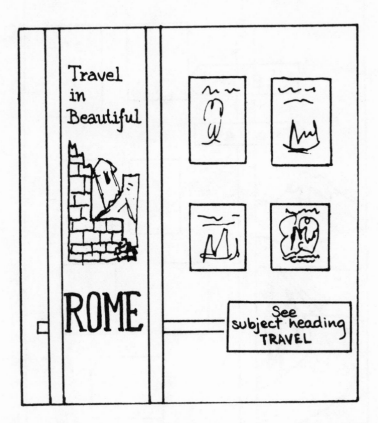

This travel design is very easy to do, since the attractor is a commercial travel poster which may sometimes be obtained from a travel agency, or purchased from many stores having posters at a nominal cost.

The board was first covered with white paper. The poster was bordered with a contrasting color, and the same color used for a baseline running to the "see" notice.

Upper-grade children admire these posters, and some are great collectors of them. They do serve as very effective attracting agents.

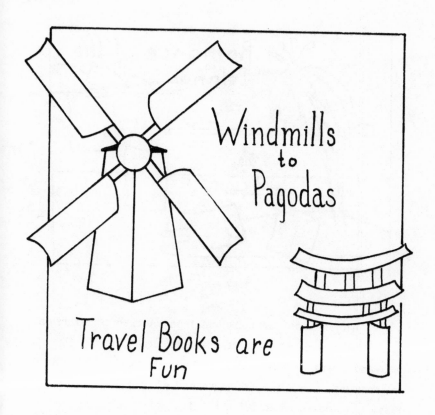

This was originally done as a poster. Later the parts were cut from construction paper, mounted on a light gray surface and used as a bulletin board.

An unexpected benefit was derived when a number of children had to ask for help in locating travel books--so occurred the need and the opportunity to teach the use of the card catalog.

All of these parts are cut from colored construction paper and mounted to a light blue surface. The sky line was added with a felt-tip pen. The palm trees on the far island were drawn in with brown and green felt-tip pens since they were too small to cut out. The palm fronds on the tree in the foreground should be slightly curled before mounting to the surface.

The caption was done with a black felt-tip pen.

Similar motifs of any country or geographical area may be easily designed and used with equal success.

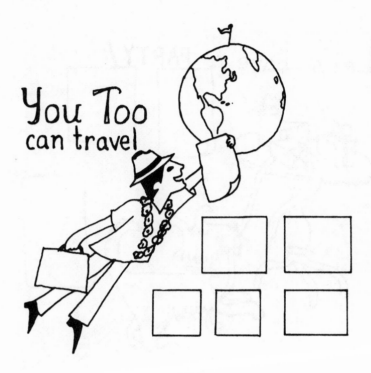

This is a simple black-on-white cartoon. The entire
design can be placed in the opaque projector, enlarged to the
desired size and copied onto the white surface with a black
felt-tip pen.

If desired, the design can be improved by cutting the
globe from light blue paper, and cementing green paper con-
tinents in place.

Another catchy caption sometimes used reads "Wait
For Me!"

This design was used to advertise books on parties and recreation in general.

The design was first enlarged to size and traced on a white background. The "gifts," ribbon, and dog were colored with crayon. The table was simply outlined with a black felt-tip pen. The caption was also lettered with a felt-tip pen.

This particular design has been done as a simple black-on-white cartoon, but it has proven more effective with some color.

Actual items, except for the paper ice cream cone, were used in the construction of this board. If these items are not available, paper streamers may be cut from crepe paper, and a hat and cone made from construction paper. The caption was added to the gray background with a wide nibbed felt-tip pen in black.

Though this board could be built from attractors simply cut from paper and mounted to the surface, it proves to be far less attractive than when done in dimension. The added time to construct the items is well spent.

When placed on a regular bulletin board, the parts
of this little owl shown here in black may be painted in any
contrasting color directly onto the background.   The colors
used really make little difference.   The caption should be
either painted in a complementary color, or cut from paper.

When placed on a blank wall, the same technique is
used, except the figure and caption will have to be trimmed
out before mounting with photographer's wax or Stik-Taks.

This funny little fellow also makes an interesting
poster.

The space was first covered with red construction
paper.   The shelves for the models were small white box
covers stapled to the space.   The caption was cut from silver
wrapping paper, and the book jackets were added.

This simple design used model cars loaned to the library by a youngster who built them.   Models of most any
subject the librarian wished to advertise are available, and
could be used.

Experience has proven designs that use items of
realia or models to be among the most effective.

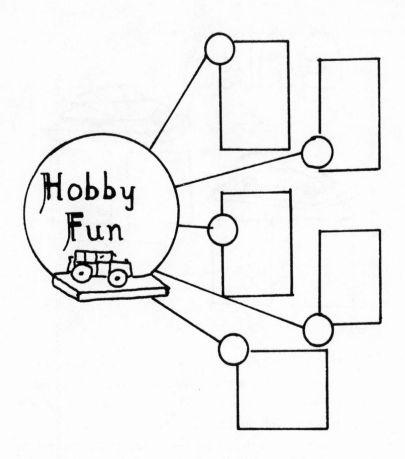

A shoebox shelf makes a mount for the model, while the red paper disk with the black caption provides a background. Yarn was used to connect the attractor with the small disks of different colors mounted over the book jackets.

Two or three shelves could be used displaying different hobbies and of course objects other than a model car could be used.

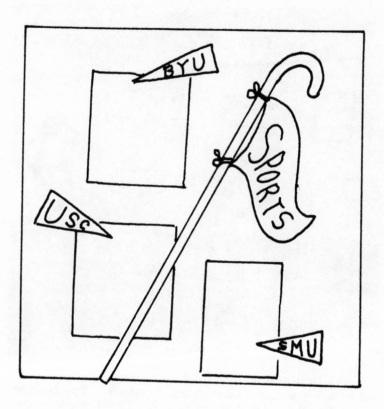

A toy cane with a cloth flag was used for the large object, and small college streamers borrowed from some of the children were added to help fill out the design.

These could all be cut from construction paper and lettered, and would be just as effective. When cut from construction paper, the cane should be raised from the board on small blocks to make it stand out. The background color should be any neutral color that will contrast with the streamers.

   I first covered the space with white craft paper. I
built the boy's face from construction paper. The book he
is reading was a sheet of brown paper folded to represent a
book. The bottom corners were cemented to the space.
Two strips of masking tape held the top of the book away
from the space to give a 3-D effect. The caption was cut
from red construction paper except "HAIR RAISERS" which
was done with a black felt pen.

   Instead of book jackets I printed titles of my favorites
on white paper, matted them on brown and mounted. I arranged some of the titles on top of the book shelf. This
type of display was good because it was a change from usual
book jackets, and the kids didn't have any trouble finding
mystery titles to read.

                              Jeannie Morine
                              5th Grade
                              East Lake School

This long-tailed nibbler may be done as a cartoon, but he is more effective when cut from light gray paper. His sweater and pants could be in the school colors. The racquet should be brown and all detail lines are easily added with a black felt-tip pen. Mounted with a dark blue caption on a white background, he is sure to attract attention to the material on display.

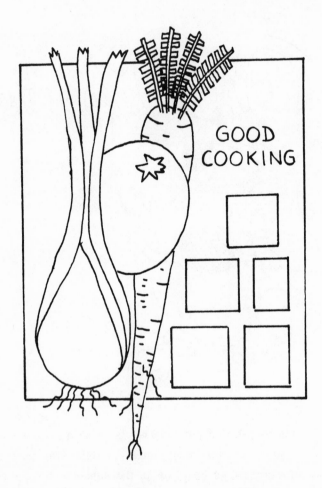

This design and the one following are almost identical, and are both used here to demonstrate how slight changes can be made in a design to change its appearance.

The onion is white with green outer leaves. The tomato is, of course, red with a green top, and the carrot is orange with the same color green top as the tomato. These were cut from construction paper and necessary roots and other lines drawn in with a black felt-tip pen.

The design was mounted on a beige surface, with the caption printed in black ink.

This design is essentially the same as the preceding page except that the vegetables were changed to fruit.

Here an apple, orange and banana were cut from construction paper and used, but any fruit shapes could be used.

This is a very striking board when it is mounted over a black background. The tent roof was cut from beige construction paper, and the scalloped edges were different colors of patterned cloth. The book jackets were trimmed and mounted side by side to form the side walls of the tent. A red flag topped off the display.

The caption was lettered across the space with a wide felt-tip black pen.

If various bits of fabric are not available, the scallops may be cut from wallpaper samples, colored advertising or decorative wrapping paper.

The scallops should be cemented to the underside of the tent roof before mounting over the top of the book jackets.

The blockhouses were cut from brown paper and all
decoration done with a black felt-tip pen. The stockade was
then cut, decorated and raised from the space on small
blocks, and the book jackets added.

This was a small size board, but it could be enlarged
and more book jackets added if this were necessary.

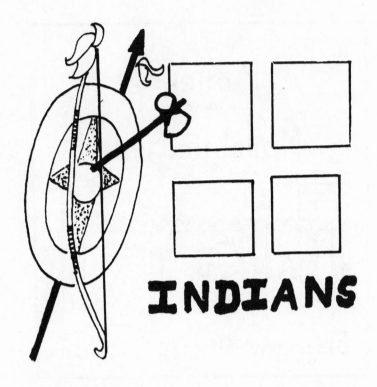

Great care must be taken in advertising materials dealing with any ethnic group. This particular design has never met with any objection from the Indian community.

The design was placed in the opaque projector, enlarged to size, traced and painted with bright colored tempera paints. The caption was painted with red tempera on a white background.

If models of the actual items were available, these could be used with possible greater effectiveness. Perhaps some students studying Indians might take this on as a class project.

This design used a flower cut from different colored bits of paper and cemented together. The bee was added with a black felt-tip pen as was the caption and flight path lines.

The design also may be constructed from a very large paper or plastic flower if one is available.

This is one of the easiest of the more successful designs, and one that children have frequently "borrowed" and teachers have utilized in their work.

When used for older children, this design may be simply drawn as a cartoon, and will prove very attractive. When done for younger children, or if time permits, it is even more successful cut from construction paper, or painted onto the surface. Any colors may be used, though the cowboy's rope should be a length of yarn or fairly heavy string or cord.

At Eastlake School, we usually paint the parts of the figure onto a light gray or yellow background, and use pinback white letters for the caption.

Here the design is used to advertise titles dealing with ranch life and history. It has also been used with captions reading, "Research Round-Up," "I Like Horses," and "New Books, Pardner."

The design also works well as a poster with the message inside the rope loop which can be made larger, or relocated on the design.

Chapter 9

SPECIAL DAYS AND SEASONS

This is one of the few areas in display work that offers many ideas to the librarian. Much of the professional
literature will offer some suggestions for holiday use, and
commercial advertising at these times of the year may also
offer some suggestions, and, possibly, some materials.

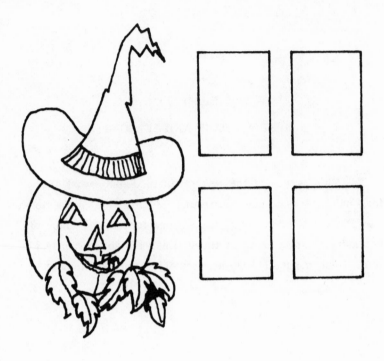

The friendly pumpkin was cut from orange construction paper with yellow paper cemented behind the cut out portions of the eye, nose and mouth.   The inside of the eyes,
nose and mouth that are exposed, were lightly shaded with
a brown crayon and outlined with a black felt-tip pen.   The
leaves were cut from green metallic wrapping paper, while
the black paper hat had a hatband cut from the same material.

     This design was more effective with the upper grades and
in the professional library than it was with the youngsters.

     This design is also easily adapted to poster display.

When used at Halloween time, the caption is cut from orange paper and mounted on a black background.

When used at other times during the year, any complementary colors may be used with the exception of pastel shades which are not bold enough for the theme.

A deep blue sky and gray fence were first placed on the space. The owl was cut from brown paper with yellow and black paper eyes, and pinned to the surface. The pumpkin was cut from orange paper with yellow eyes, nose and mouth. The bat was black, and folded down the center of the body so the wings would stand out from the space. The stars were added with a bit of aluminum paint and a fine watercolor brush. Gummed stars from the supply cupboard could also be used.

The book jackets were lightly curled and added last. The display was very effective.

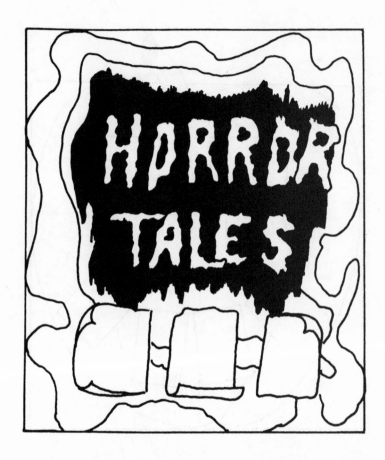

Green paper makes up the background for this design. The white paper free-form shape with an added black detail line was mounted next. Black paper was then cut to shape, and the caption cut from it. This was then mounted over the white paper.

When the curled book jackets were added the whole thing came to a somewhat sickly life, but the children loved it.

The author has always felt that the attractiveness of this design when used at Halloween time might lie in the fact that it does not rely on the usual motifs of the holiday, and being different, is more attractive.

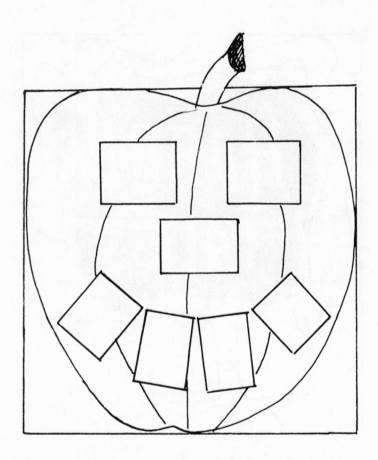

If the librarian is pressed for time, this simple, if
not inspiring design may be the answer for his Halloween or
fall theme.

The orange pumpkin was mounted on gray paper. The
facial features were book jackets, and pumpkin lines were
added with a black felt-tip pen.

This design uses wire coat hangers for the bodies of the witch and the cat, though the cat's must be bent into shape. Construction paper heads and broom complete the attractor for this display. The caption was cut from orange construction paper and mounted to the white background.

If desired, a black paper shape may be cut and mounted inside the coat hanger for more color.

THANKSGIVING

TURKEYS

PILGRIMS

HOLIDAYS

This design was no real design at all, but it did improve the circulation of titles on the three subjects related
to Thanksgiving.

The space was first covered with a very pale pink
paper. The lettering was then put on with a wide felt-tip
pen in brown. The lettering could be placed on contrasting
strips of paper and these mounted to the space if more color
were needed.

The book jackets were added last.

Any topic that can be divided into parts may be advertised in this manner. The design is especially adaptable
to such general topics as Careers or Geography which have
many possible sub-topics.

This design may be done as a black and white cartoon, but it is much more effective done in colors, either painted onto the white background, or cut from colored paper.

The turkey had a blue head, yellow bill and red wattle. The neck was dark brown and the body, light brown. The wing was black, white and dark brown at the tips. The tail was done in the same colors. The apples, pumpkin and grapes were done in their natural colors. The caption was lettered with a black felt-tip pen.

This particular design worked best in either the professional library, or with older students.

Four coat hangers, two pie plates (paper) and some
bits of construction paper make up this design. The space
was first covered with lime green paper. A brown strip was
then added, and the caption was painted onto this with thick
white poster paint. The clothes hangers were then stapled
in place, and the pie plate faces with details already cemented
in place, was added last. Book jackets or audio-visual materials being advertised were arranged on the space to complete the display.

This type of display can be mounted on a blank wall
by first building it on a large sheet of tagboard and mounting
the tagboard to the wall with photographer's wax, double
faced masking tape, or masking tape loops. Never use scotch
tape. It may pull the finish off the wall, or leave unsightly
marks at best.

This design does not use any book jackets, being used simply as a decoration. There is no reason why it couldn't be used to advertise titles too.

Because of the time required to do this one, it becomes an excellent project for the library club or the art department.

The tree is built from folded, green tagboard. Cardboard tubes are cut to the same width, and some are painted in Christmas colors and others are wrapped with decorative paper. These are then all glued into place within the Christmas tree form.

The candles were built from construction paper rolled into a tube, and the base was made from folded construction paper the same width as the tree and candles. The entire design was mounted on black paper, and the caption brushed in with aluminum paint.

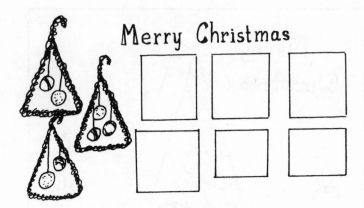

This design uses three coat hangers, some tinsel rope in gold or any other color available, Christmas ornaments and some bits of narrow ribbon.

The coat hangers are bent to shape and wrapped with the tinsel rope. The ornaments are hung in the space created by the coat hanger with the ribbon.

These are then hung in the bulletin board space and the book jackets added. The caption may be done with a felt-tip pen, but is more effective if done with a very lightweight tinsel cord dropped on pins in the shape of the letters. The background may be any contrasting material that has a flat finish, such as construction paper.

White construction paper figures, decorated with tempera paint, are mounted to a red surface to which a green fir tree has already been attached.   Thin straws were used for the banner poles, and the banner, reading Merry Christmas, was strung between these.

If stiff enough straws can not be located, then the banner may be partially sculptured, added to the surface and the poles painted in with paint or a brown felt-tip marking pen.

One year, the library was able to obtain three real dolls in proper costume to use for this display.   It made a very striking effect.

Designs of this type may be used to advertise material or simply as on oversized greeting card design for decoration.

This may be done as a cartoon; it may be traced onto
the surface and colored for added interest; or the figures
may be traced, cut out, decorated, and then placed on the
surface on two sizes of blocks so that the figures stand on three
different planes.

Decoration may be done with paints or inks, cut paper,
fabric or decorative wrapping paper.

Designs such as this are common around Christmas,
and may be borrowed from greeting cards, advertising, design idea publications and coloring books. Many of these
can be adapted to library use with few problems.

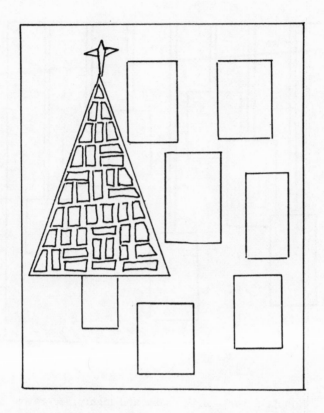

This Christmas design may look rather complicated, but it is really very simple and easy to do. The space was first covered with black paper. The tree was cut from green construction paper, and a book jacket used for the trunk. Metallic foil wrapping paper in different colors was cut into patches and cemented to the tree and an aluminum foil star was added to the tip.

The tree was mounted on small blocks to raise it from the surface and then the book jackets were added.

Three of these trees in different sizes can be arranged to make a most decorative holiday motif without any book jackets.

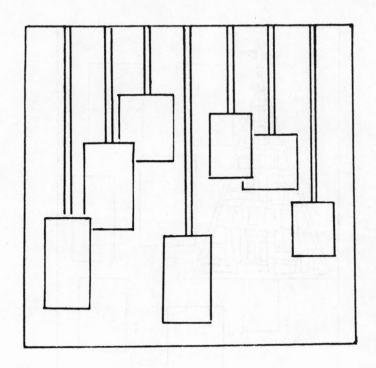

This is a very quick, easy and highly decorative design for Christmas. The brightest colors of decorative ribbon should be used, and it should be wide, up to 2-1/2 to 3 inches if possible.

The space is covered with aluminum foil. The book jackets are attached to the ribbon, and the ribbon cut to various lengths to allow the book jackets to hang at various heights.

If there is too much draft to allow the jackets to hang in place, the jackets will also have to be pinned to the board.

White construction paper Wise Men ride black paper camels across tan colored sands, guided by a star shape painted on the blue surface with a bit of metallic aluminum paint.

The design is quite easily done and, though traditional, generally effective.

This design used a party hat, horn and confetti rib-
bons in its construction, with little patches cut from metallic
foils for added color. These items could be constructed
from paper or one can simply cut the shapes out and mount
them. The "73" was cut from black construction paper and
mounted to the white surface. The caption was lettered in
with a black felt-tip pen.

The green stem and branches were first put onto the pale blue space with a green felt-tip pen. Several sheets of red construction paper were placed on top of each other and a number of red hearts were cut. These were cut in two slightly different sizes to make the board more interesting, and glued to the surface. The book jackets, some slightly curled, were added last.

This Valentine tree has been done in large scale by using green yarn for stems held to a blank wall by bits of photographer's wax. The Valentines and book jackets were added to create a very decorative display.

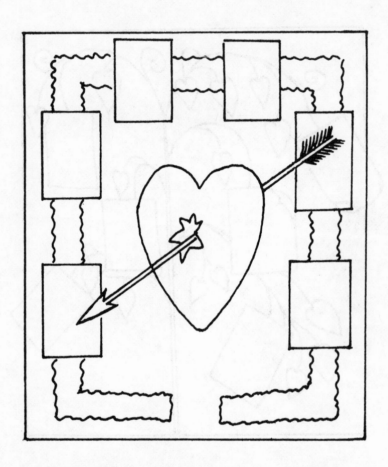

This is quite traditional but the children like it.   The space was first covered with white paper.   A streamer of crepe paper was cut and the edges pulled to crinkle it.   This was then pinned to the board to make a contrasting tie-in for the book jackets.   The red heart with the hole torn in the center was then added.   The yellow arrow with the brown feathers and tip was added last.   No caption was needed with this board.

The board can be improved somewhat by placing small blocks behind the heart and arrow to raise them from the space a bit and so give a feeling of depth to the display.

Valentine's Day is so traditional, it is quite difficult
to develop much originality in designs. This design did receive some added attractiveness by constructing the heart
from a piece of red and white checked material. The flowers were cut from a small patterned purple and white print,
and the stems and grass line were added with a green felt-
tip pen. The attractor was added to a background of pale
pink paper, and the caption added with a red felt-tip pen.

The green metallic wrapping paper hat is the main attractor on this board. The black band and the gold or silver buckle add contrast. The shamrock shapes were cut from light green paper and the caption was added with a black felt-tip pen.

Though this design used a light gray background, any contrasting color could be used.

Since this topic suggests Ireland, it can also be used for history, geography or travel related to this country.

This big white bunny with pink nose and ear linings and large blue eyes stands on a base of green paper grass and flowers. The book jackets he holds suggest Easter Week reading.

A background of almost any darker color will make him stand out in sharp contrast. The entire design is very effective with both older and younger children.

When little "Miss Stuck-up" (as the children dubbed her) is used in upper grades, she is effective as a simple black-on-white cartoon design, but when used with younger children she should be colored.

Though painting her is satisfactory, she becomes a better attractor if her dress is made from some brightly colored material. The material may be either cemented flat to the surface, or it may be loose to suggest shape.

Though a rabbit is traditionally white, the design may be any color; it is fun to break with tradition occasionally and listen to the children's comments. Sometimes it helps the design as an attractor.

The white construction paper bunny is first mounted on a pink, gray or black background. Book jackets come next. The cart, cut from construction paper and decorated with tempera paint, is mounted on small blocks and added next. Last are the construction paper flowers and greenery, also mounted on blocks to raise them from the surface.

This design takes a bit longer to construct than most of those illustrated in this title, but its success in boosting circulation is well worth the effort.

Occasionally it is possible to locate a large advertising display similar to this in design that can be cut, trimmed and adapted to library work. Such items should be saved for future use if possible.

The space for this design was first covered with light
blue construction paper. The tree trunks were cut from brown
paper and added next. The foliage was cut from yellow, red and
tan paper, the yellow being used for the foreground, the red for
the middle tree, and the tan for the last one, which doesn't have
a trunk showing. The foliage was then mounted along with the
book jackets. The caption was cut from dark brown paper and
mounted last.

This design could be painted onto the surface, but cutting
the parts from paper is quicker.

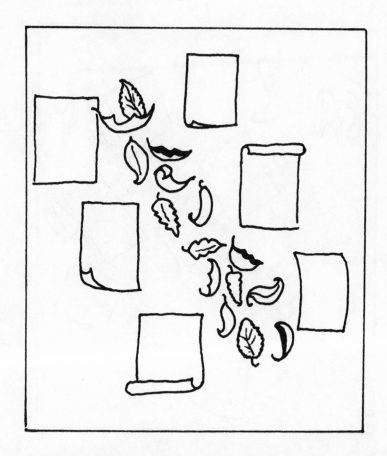

This fall board is quite decorative and easy to construct. Autumn-colored leaves are cut from construction paper, lightly sculptured, and pinned to the space which has first been covered with a light green paper. The book jackets are also slightly sculptured before mounting.

No caption is required with this design.

If the librarian has an assortment of plastic leaves in fall colors for use, these will work just as well and save the time of cutting them out of paper.

This design is half cartoon and half cut paper. The black "wind" lines were added to the white background with a black felt-tip pen. The leaves were cut from construction paper in autumn colors and pinned to the board. The book jackets were bent, curled and added. The caption was cut from brown paper.

This is a design that young library aides like to construct, and it takes only a few minutes. Care must be taken, however, in curling the book jackets, to preserve their readability.

Designs depicting a scene, such as this winter theme, are almost always good, though they may take a little longer to construct. This one started with a light blue background. The distant hills were cut from white paper and mounted to the space. The lake was left blue. The snow along the bottom of the board was then cut from white paper and mounted. Next, the log cabin with its snow-covered roof, and the trees behind it as well as those in the lower right-hand corner, were cut and positioned. The last to be mounted were the dark green trees in the foreground. These were mounted so as to conceal part of the left side of the cabin.

No caption is needed with this board, though one could be added if the librarian felt it necessary.

Children of most any age love the humor of this design and it is easy to complete. The space was first covered with light blue paper. The snow bank behind the book jackets was cut from white paper and mounted to the space. The "Hole" was colored in with a dark blue felt-tip pen and the stick holding the sign was done with a yellow pen. The sign was a bit of white paper with the caption done in red.

The hats on the book jackets were cut from colored construction paper and pinned in place over the book jackets. The legs and skates were drawn in with a black felt-tip pen.

The main caption was cut from white paper and mounted to the board.

This winter design uses a background of light gray paper. The snow at the bottom was cut from white paper and
mounted in place. The snowman was cut from white paper and
the scarf painted red. When mounted, the snowman was outlined
with a black felt-tip pen to make him stand out. The eyes,
mouth and buttons were also inked in with the pen. The caption
was lettered in with a black felt-tip pen as were the trees on the
right-hand side.

The entire board gives a very cold feeling. If it proves
too much so, the background may be changed to light blue.

This simple little design is very easy to complete.
The background was first covered with a very light pastel
green paper. Six patches of pink paper were placed together and
cut into the flower shapes. As these were mounted in the space,
a small bit of white paper was cemented in the center of each.
The leaves of the smaller plant were cut in one piece from a
deep green paper and mounted to the board. The larger leaves
were cut individually from a light green paper and lightly sculptured before mounting to the surface. The stems and ground
line were added with a green felt-tip pen. The caption was lettered in brown with a felt-tip pen and the two flowers were also
outlined with brown before mounting.

The addition of book jackets completes the display.

Springtime... Reading Time

The bird may not be too well designed but children find him funny. He was drawn onto beige paper and painted blue with red tail band, neck ruff, beak, and legs. The limb on which he is standing is deep brown while the flowers are pink with white centers. The caption was done with blue paint.

The book jackets were lightly curled and placed to follow the sight line in the design.

And here he is again, this time wearing a different suit of clothes.

A good use for these repeater designs is to use them throughout the library and other display areas at the same time, each design changed as these illustrations show. It is not suggested that this unity in display throughout the area be a regular custom of the library, but occasionally reinforcement is gained by the repetition.

This silly little bird was first traced onto the white paper surface. The leaves were painted green and the jonquils yellow, with black construction lines where necessary. The little bird was painted light blue with a black wing and tail and a yellow beak. His eye was put on with a black felt-tip pen.

The caption was added with a black felt-tip pen.

Most any colors could be used. If time is no factor, the design could be cut out and mounted on blocks for added interest, or the design treated as a simple black-and-white cartoon design.

When used with upper grades the cartoon design is quite effective, but for primary children, the color is quite essential if the board is to prove attractive.

This chapter offers a few designs that have been planned specifically for the primary grades. Since all of these designs have a great flexibility in use, most could be used in any area of the school, but they will have special appeal to the younger children.

175

Mother Goose was traced onto a sheet of paper and painted; the paper was then cut out and mounted over a dark surface.

The feathered areas were painted gray with an orange bill. The bonnet and scarf were painted white with shading added with a black felt-tip pen. The dress was painted green and the book yellow with black lettering. Of course, any combination of bright colors could be used. Younger children like this design.

The seal may be painted onto a white or light blue background, or he may be cut from black paper. If he is cut from black paper, the construction lines should be cut out to give the added detail. If he is painted, care should be taken not to paint these areas. The words were added to the background with a felt-tip pen.

The design was used to advertise humor and joke books, but could be used for sea life, circus life, or as an attractor for a general topic board.

Illustrative materials from children's books of all kinds make good bulletin board designs. <u>Tuggy the Tug Boat</u> and <u>Loopy the Airplane</u> are just as attractive as an illustration of one of the nursery rhymes.

This particular one was cut from construction paper. The cow was brown with black horns, hooves, tail and bell collar. The eyes and nose were pink with detail lines added with a felt-tip pen. The bell was cut from a scrap of gold wrapping paper.

The moon was cut from yellow paper with the eye added by use of a black felt-tip pen. The moon was raised from the surface by the use of small bits of cardboard tube.

The background was light green, and the caption was added with a brown felt-tip pen. Book jackets were scattered around the figures to complete the design.

This juggling clown is wearing a costume and hat cut
from red on white polka-dot material. His hair was brown
paper, his face, mitts, and shoes white construction paper.
A blue eye, red nose and mouth completed him. The design
and the book jackets were mounted on a black background
for greater contrast.

This design is also excellent for a blank wall, and
can easily be adapted to poster work.

Three Blind Mice
and other songs and rhymes

Little children really like this design. The mice
were made by bending wire coat hangers into shape. When
these were stapled to the light gray surface, pink ears and
black construction paper glasses were added. The tails
were lengths of black yarn pinned in place. The caption
was added with a wide felt-tip pen in black.

Book jackets were added above the caption.

These mice should be stapled carefully to the space,
for small children will run their hands over them.

The frog was cut from green tagboard and yellow
spots were painted on.   Black construction lines were added
along with purple eyes, red mouth and white book.   The
lily pad was cut from dark green paper with the turned-up
edge a very light green cemented in place.   The whole design was mounted on a light blue surface to suggest water.

The caption is on the cover of the book.   Children
of all ages enjoy this design.

Look at these!

The action of Mrs. Crow lends an air of excitement
to the finished display whether she is done as a simple black
and white cartoon or dressed with scraps of colored cloth and
given a pair of yellow legs.

When done as a cartoon, the design may be placed in
the opaque projector, enlarged to size, copied and painted in
with black tempera paint. If more color is desired, the
apron should be left white and the head scarf painted some
bright color. The legs and the inside of the beak should be
painted a contrasting color. Perched on a brown twig with
a couple of green leaves, she becomes quite colorful. Added
interest can be achieved by constructing the head scarf from
a scrap of cloth and cementing it in place. Two or three
green plastic leaves added to the display also improve its
attractiveness.

Any way this design is completed, the addition of
some book jackets will result in a display both attractive and
interesting to younger patrons.

The gray paper elephant carrying the red sign with
the black lettering will catch the eye of most any age group.
Any neutral color will work well for the background. The
ground lines and grass clumps can be added with a green
felt-tip pen.

The design does not lend itself to a black-on-white
cartoon because there is too much mass to the elephant, and
the design simply goes unnoticed. It must be colored.

This is a very simple, though effective, design--one
which children can construct with little difficulty.

    Hippy the Hippo was constructed the same as the design on the preceding page.

    An entire parade of animals could easily be constructed on this same idea, and would prove effective. In designing these creatures it is well to keep in mind that they are more effective if they are smiley, happy, friendly creatures rather than gloomy or ugly. Even such fearful beasts as a python or a crocodile can be made funny or smiling. Remember too, that they need not approximate the actual color of the animal. Hippy was painted gray, but he could just as well have been cut from a brightly printed cloth or a wall paper sample.

This little monkey was painted onto a white background with tempera paints. He had a red hat with green trim and tassel, red jacket and blue pants. His face was light brown, while his hair was dark brown. His shoes were black. His hands were cut from brown construction paper closely matching his hair. This was necessary in order not to paint over the book jackets.

The design is effective both in a regular space as well as along a blank wall.

If both sides are painted, and a crook put in his tail to suspend him, he makes a most interesting mobile.

Though this board was used with alphabet books, it could be used for other themes.

The background for this display was gray. The apples were cut from construction paper. The leaves were also cut from construction paper, while the stems were colored in with a brown felt-tip pen. The large A was cut from red construction paper, while the rest of the caption was lettered in with a black felt-tip pen.

This design has also been done by shaping the apples from coat hangers and adding a free-formed patch of red construction paper for color. The loop end of the hanger was wrapped with brown crepe paper for the stem, and a green paper leaf cemented in place.

Apples can also be cut from large commercial advertising posters, or built from a heavy fabric. Painting them in place does not prove as effective as the cut-outs.

The background for this display was a very light blue corrugated cardboard. The mouse was cut from gray construction paper and the hair was colored black with a crayon; the insides of the ears were colored pink. This figure was then mounted in the space. The cheese was cut from yellow paper. The top of the cheese was colored red and the holes were drawn in with a black felt-tip pen. The completed board used no caption.

When used on a blank wall, a gray mouse may not contrast enough to be noticed, so he should be cut from some other color. Actually, any colors may be used and even a patterned paper is interesting.

This cartoon design was painted on the surface with the exception of the leaves, which were cut from green construction paper.

The toadstool was outlined with a brown felt-tip pen and the circles were done with a red pen. The fronds were done in green, while the fern-type leaves were outlined in purple.

The design has been used both as a simple attractor with a general topic display, and to advertise titles dealing with ferns, mosses and related plant life.

The little tiger has been done as a simple cartoon and was quite effective. He is more of an attractor if the parts shown in white are cut from orange construction paper and then cemented to dark brown or black paper to produce the stripes. The red mouth, black nose and green or black eyes may be painted on. Whiskers were added last with a black felt-tip pen.

The ground line and grass was painted on the background with green paint.

This little fellow has proven so popular that he is now in the process of being painted and cut from masonite so he can be added to the collection of circulating designs.

Though the lamb may be done in white construction paper on a black background, he is much more effective when done with cotton except for the face, which is cut from white construction paper. A real pink bow is added at his throat and blue eyes add a bit more color. The ground lines and flowers may be cut from paper or they may be painted on the surface.

Designs such as this one may be found in children's coloring books. Though these designs are not always very well drafted, they are good sources in which to search for ideas.

When used in a bulletin board space, this clown was simply painted onto a light surface with tempera paints, and the book jackets added.

When he was used on a blank wall, he was cut out after painting and mounted with photographer's wax.

To make a sad-faced clown, simply draw him with his mouth turned down.

The happy elephant taking a bath is most amusing to younger children. He was cut from gray paper with water and construction lines added with a black felt-tip pen. Mounted against a contrasting background he has proven to be a powerful attractor.

Used here, he serves merely to attract attention to a general theme. He could be used to advertise such materials as animals, Africa, India, or even health.

This little girl was built from various colors of construction paper cemented together to complete the figure, though she would be easy to trace and cut from white paper and paint. When completed, she was mounted on small blocks over a dark brown surface to which book jackets had been pinned.

No caption is needed for this design, since the type of books being advertised should be obvious from the book jackets, and there simply is no room for a caption.

Here she is carrying a frog, but she could be carrying a book, an umbrella, a kitten or anything else a little girl might carry with her.

This clown was traced onto a white surface and painted. Any colors may be used so long as they are bright.

Where this design is to be used on a blank wall, it should be cut out after it has been painted.

This design takes a little time to complete, but it is so attractive, especially to younger children, that it is worth the time, and it can be stored and used over again at later dates.

Just a simple little decoration, developed by a seventh-grade student for the primary grades at Easter time, but a most effective one. The rabbit was cut from pink paper, detail lines were added with a black felt-tip pen, and a single plastic dime-store flower was tucked into his paw. Book jackets were added to the light blue background to complete the design; no caption was needed.

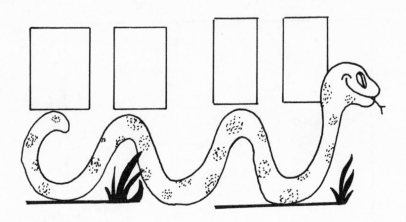

This friendly little viper was cut from white cloth
that had blotches of pink and green for decoration. The facial features were added by black felt-tip pen. An old plastic
green jewel was cemented in place for an eye.

The book jackets were first mounted on the space
which had been covered with very light blue corrugated paper.
The snake was pinned in place, and the dark green groundline
and clumps of grass were added last.

Since the snake was simply an attractor, no caption
was used for this display. This design has been used to advertise reptiles, and has been built from wallpaper as well
as cut from children's finger painting.

One librarian did this design in greens and deep blues,
opened the mouth, added fangs and a vicious expression.
Small children did not like it and she had to take it down.
Changing it to a "friendly" snake changed the attitude of the
children. This experience may lend credence to the notion
of keeping displays light and pleasant.

Embossed papers or rough textured material will work
well for this type of display if it is placed low enough for
the children to run their hands over it. They like the feel
and the tactile sensation will draw them back to the board
over and over again and help draw their attention to the interesting book jackets.

The little clown has a construction paper head, hands and feet. The rest of him was cut from red and white polka-dotted material. The hair was a bit of well-combed black yarn cemented to the top of the head before the hat was added. The white yarn from the book jackets was threaded through two holes in his hand before the figure was cemented to the contrasting background.

The little clown is as much at home on a blank wall as he is in a regular bulletin board space.

This basic design may be done as a simple cartoon, or the parts may be cut from construction paper, or the design may be painted. It is very effective in any of these media.

The rabbit may be just about any color and wear just about any colored clothing. The design works equally well in a regular bulletin board space or along a blank wall. Done on a smaller scale, it makes an effective poster display.

This is a basic cartoon figure. Change the tail and ears, add a stripe or spots and you change the animal to something else. Change the hair and use a skirt instead of pants and you change the figure from male to female. Children enjoy these cartoon-type figures and they are very easy and quick to complete.

Though this design is used in the East Lake Library as a simple cartoon drawing, the figure can be cut from paper or painted. He may be mounted on blocks or mounted directly to the surface.

Every librarian should have several of these basic cartoon shapes in his idea file, available for circulation to the student body and the staff.

Change the tail, ears or other basic parts and the design becomes another animal to be used as an attractor in display work.

This friendly fellow may be done as a cartoon, copied and painted, or cut from construction paper. In our library he is cut from heavy tagboard. The blue denim pants and white cloth sweater help set off his brown painted body. His mouth was painted red, his nose black, and his eyes blue.

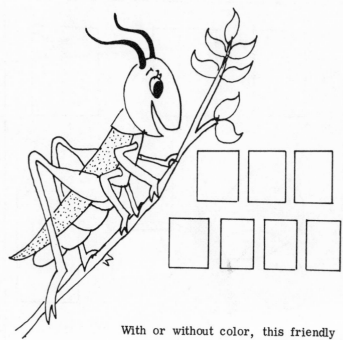

With or without color, this friendly little fellow is always a powerful attractor and may be used as a simple design, or to advertise titles on insects or any other related topic.

He was traced onto light tagboard, cut out, and painted. The wings were painted green, and the rest, yellow, to which a touch of brown was added. The eye was white and the pupil green. The detail lines were added with a black felt-tip pen after the paint was dry.

A twig to which construction paper leaves were glued was first mounted to the surface, which had been covered with beige paper. The addition of the bug and book jackets completed the display.

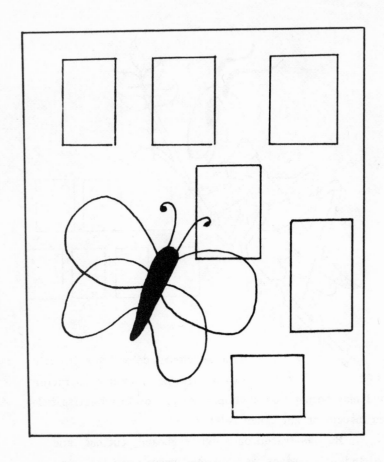

The butterfly may be done in a number of different ways. Since this one was added to the materials circulation library for use by the staff, it was constructed from wire coat hangers. The body was cut from heavy tagboard to which a piece of red metallic foil had been glued before cutting. The antennae were long jumbo pipe cleaners.

This display was built on a light gray background, though most any color could be used.

Chapter 11

Don't forget...

Charge a good book today

This is a very common type of design best suited for poster work. This may be done as a black-on-white drawing. The hand may be cut from colored construction paper and mounted on a background of contrasting color, or painted onto a surface.

Some other captions might read:

    Return your books on time
    Avoid a fine

    Library Club
    Tuesday at three

    Pictures help your
    report.

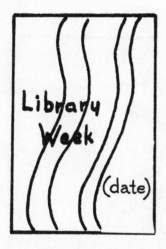

These posters were all painted on tagboard in bright colors with tempera paint.   The two bottom designs were cut out after painting.

This poster was drawn on white cardboard. The book covers were lightly shaded with brown crayon. The world was an illustration cut from a discarded social studies book and cemented in place. The captions were done with a black felt-tip pen, as were the lines suggesting pages.

Traced onto tagboard and painted, this design becomes an attractive poster.

When done on a larger scale and set in an array of book jackets, it becomes an attractive bulletin board.

A large stuffed doll or animal may also be used in place of the figure.

The caption, of course, goes on the sign.

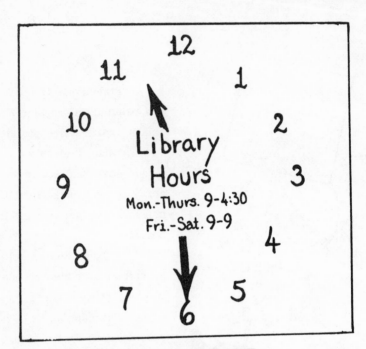

Library
Hours
Mon.-Thurs. 9-4:30
Fri.-Sat. 9-9

Going to summer school?

Maybe we
can help with
materials...

NEED ANY
PICTURES...?

Discards to be
cut up for your own use